Radio, TV, MOTHER EARTH &ME
Memories of a Hollywood Life
JOEL RAPP

Other Books by Joel Rapp

Gifts from our Garbage

Mother Earth's Hassle-Free Indoor Plant Book

Grow With your Plants the Mother Earth Hassle-Free Way

Fabulous Fish

Let's Get Growing

Mother Earth's Hassle-Free Vegetable Cookbook

Mother Earth's Vegetarian Feasts

Mother Earth's Coloring Album

Mr. Mother Earth's Most Rewarding Houseplants

Dear Mother Earth

Radio, TV, MOTHER EARTH

&ME Memories of a Hollywood Life
JOEL RAPP

BearManor Media
2004

Radio, TV, Mother Earth & Me: Memories of a Hollywood Life
© 2004 by Joel Rapp.
All rights reserved.

Published in the USA by

BearManor Media
P. O. Box 750
Boalsburg, PA 16827

bearmanormedia.com

Cover design by Steven Hitter
Photo by Zoë Melzack
Typesetting and layout by John Teehan

ISBN—1-59393-005-4

To THE PATRONS
OF THE BRENTWOOD
LIBRARY —
Hope you enjoy!

Juel Rapp

4/18/04

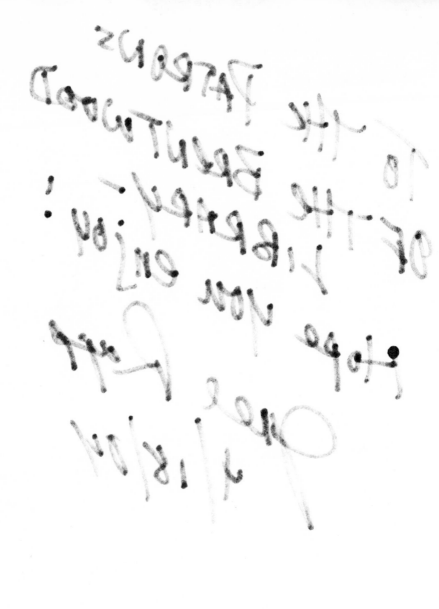

This book is dedicated to my adorable grand-daughters, Hannah and Sophie, presently 5 and 3 years old, with the hope they will read it when they're older so they will get a sense of who their "Poppy" was (is) and give them a look at the times in which I grew up and lived.

I would also like to thank everybody else who played a part in making my life so exciting and memorable, which includes everybody whose name is included in these pages and a few more besides. A special thanks to my wife, Suzie, who encouraged me to write it all down, and an extra special thanks to my Mom and Dad for making my life possible in the first place.

Table of Contents

Foreword by Roger Corman i

A Little Taste of History 1

The Beginning 7

Dad Fiddles While Mom Births 17

V-J Day In Hollywood 21

An Eddie Cantor Vignette 25

Fanny Brice 27

School Days 31

I Will Go To Korea! (Not!) 41

Show-biz, Here I Come! 45

Me and the Mob 49

The Ghost of Lenny Bruce 53

Goodbye Bachelor Days—the First Time 55

Our Hitch With *McHale's Navy* 59

Ernest Borgnine Exposed 63

Bob Hope the Actor—Not!! 65

Match Please, Darling 67

The Wedding of the Century 71

Golfing With Gable 75

The Birth of 'Mother Earth' 77

How a Martian Got Me Into Plants 85

Never Judge a Book By Its Cover 87

Ruth Buzzi 91

Author, Author! 93

The Man Who Loved Bromeliads 101

I Loved Lucy (and better yet, she loved me!) 103

Wolfgang—And I Don't Mean Mozart 107

The Death of Mother Earth 109

Born Again! 113

New York, New York, It's a Wonderful Town 119

The Producer 125

An Adventure In Hong Kong 129

"Saturday Morning Live!" 133

My Regis Years 137

If You Knew Suzie 141

California, Here We Come! 145

A Family Feud 149

The Travel Section 153

Home Sweet Home 173

Foreword
by Roger Corman

I first met Joel Rapp in 1958, not long after I had broken into the movie business, first as a producer and then as a producer-director of low budget, youth-oriented films. All these pictures made money, so I decided to invest the profits into launching my own production company, Filmgroup. In addition to making pictures myself, I planned to increase the company's production slate by investing in a few pictures which I would executive produce. Joel, who was recommended by a friend, came to me with an idea about a nerdy but brilliant high-school student who masterminds a daring robbery in order to impress the school homecoming queen. I liked the idea, I was impressed by Joel's enthusiasm and quick wit, and I figured it didn't hurt that Joel's father, Philip Rapp, creator of The Bickersons and Baby Snooks, was a comedy writing legend. So I gave Joel a shot at writing and directing *High School Big Shot*. He did a terrific job, the picture did well, and my relationship with Joel was under way.

Over the next decades we made several more movies together, all genre pictures designed to appeal to youthful audiences. Joel is an outstanding writer. In particular, he is a brilliant comedy writer. I believe that humor is an essential ingredient of almost any picture, including drama, science-fiction or horror, so over the years I called on Joel many times to punch up scripts by adding jokes and funny lines. Joel is the master of the quick comeback or witty aside. Here's an example: I was explaining to a new, bright young assistant that although I like humor in a picture, I believe that comedy is the most difficult art, demanding the highest level of skill from writer, director, and cast, thus I have made very few full-out comedies. "At least not intentionally," Joel interjected.

Joel's directorial skills are as sharp as his humor. Although he never had much of a budget to work with, and some of the scripts I assigned him to direct were, at best, only average, his direction showed an instinctive understanding of the medium. Had Joel decided to pursue directing instead of writing, I think he would have joined the pantheon of directors such as Francis Coppola, Martin Scorsese, Ron Howard, Jonathan Demme, Joe Dante, and James Cameron—young directors who got their start with me and went on to legendary Hollywood success.

You'll find entertaining stories of our work together in this memoir: our adventures in Puerto Rico where Joel wrote and directed *The Battle of Blood Island* (based on a Philip Roth novella), while I made a movie called *It Came from Beneath the Sea*, and our couple of months in Europe making *The Wild Racers* in which we shot a picture moving from country to country following the Formula One Auto races. The thing that stands out in my memory is the day after the picture wrapped and we were going over the final expenditures. I always allowed 10% of the budget for unexplained expenses—petty cash unaccounted for, petty thievery, etc., and was pleased to see that the unexplained expenses for *The Wild Racers* amounted to a mere 5% of our hundred-thousand dollar budget. When I congratulated Joel on keeping the figure down to only five thousand dollars, he shook his head in bewilderment. "I wonder who got the other thousand?" he said, and to this day I don't know whether or not he was kidding.

Although Joel and I were very close friends as well as working associates, I really never knew the full extent of his incredibly exciting life until I read these memoirs. The story of the rise and fall of Mother Earth is fodder for a highly dramatic movie, and the anecdotes dating back to his childhood in Beverly Hills and subsequent years in and around showbusiness are each, in their own way, a delight to read. I'm sure you'll enjoy this book as much as I did.

A Little Taste of History

The Chinese have a saying: "You should be born in interesting times." Well, I have been around during eight decades (so far) on this planet and I must say they have been more than interesting—they've been incredible. The things that I've seen, the events that have taken place, the scientific and technological advances that have been made are quite simply mind-boggling. For instance, when I was born, in the 1930s, air-travel was a brand new experience. I remember taking a trip from L.A. to New York with my Dad on an airplane that had bunks like a railroad sleeper-car and took twenty hours to get to the East Coast—with lots of stops along the way.

There was no television in the 30s, but radio was huge. There were tons of shows on every day on three major network stations—lots of 15 minute soap operas, comedy shows, westerns, mysteries, news programs...I grew up listening to the radio and there was something very special about being able to imagine the people and places they were re-creating. Many was the day that I faked a cold so I could stay home and listen to *Pepper Young's Family*, or *One Life to Live*...Doctors still made house-calls, and movies were a dime. Many people still had "ice boxes" instead of the new-fangled refrigerators, and although they had abandoned their horse-drawn carts for trucks, ice-men still made regular deliveries. Compared to today, prices back then were ridiculous. I have a 1938 menu someplace from Musso & Frank's Grill in Hollywood. There's not a thing over a dollar on the entire bill of fare. Gasoline was ten-cents a gallon and a pack of cigarettes cost 25 cents. In other words, things were very, very cheap back then. A man making twenty-five dollars a week was considered to be doing very well. (I say man, because very few women worked in those days.) Given all that, you can imagine how rich my father was during those years when he was making 7500 dollars a week!

The 1940s brought World War II, with its rationing and belt-tightening and War Bond Drives and women coming into the workplace in factories that churned out airplanes and tanks and guns and ships twenty-four hours a day, seven days a week. It was an incredibly patriotic time, and the American people joined together against the common enemies, Germany, Japan, and Italy, and thus rose to the occasion. The period after the war brought great growth to Los Angeles, essentially in the San Fernando Valley. When my father bought that two-and-a-half-acre ranch back in 1938 or '39, the Valley was virtually deserted. Right after the war, tons of GI housing sprung up and a military veteran could buy a nice three-bedroom house for nothing down and very few dollars a month. I sigh when I think that those little houses, which sold for around ten-thousand bucks, are now worth at least two-hundred to three-hundred thousand dollars. The site of the ranch, for which my folks paid 40 thousand dollars including the cost of all the buildings, stables, the pool, etc., was subsequently divided into five half-acre estates which today would cost over a million dollars apiece.

The '50s—often called "The Beat Generation"—were pretty bland around these parts. The nickname came from a smallish group of artists, musicians and poets who hung around coffee houses, primarily in New York and Los Angeles, and because of their laid-back style came to be known as "Beatnicks." Eisenhower was President, the Korean conflict was the decade's major War, but all in all people had it pretty good during those years. Men went to work, women stayed home and took care of the household. Television made its breakthrough and almost everybody had a black-and-white TV set upon which to watch Milton Berle, "Mr. Television," on Tuesday nights. There wasn't much crime during those years—at least it didn't seem like it—and nobody, including us, ever locked their doors either at home or in their cars. The music changed, as Rock and Roll became the staple of young people everywhere, led by the "The King," Elvis Presley, and I graduated from USC, started my writing career, and married Lisa and Danielle's mother.

The '60s brought a whole new sensibility. The Beatles came to America, John F. Kennedy was the young, handsome President who was assassinated after only two years at the helm and mostly because of the opposition to the Vietnam War, an entire new sub-culture was born. They were young men and women—mostly college age—who rose up to protest the rules and regulations of the Establishment, now being led by President Johnson. Anybody over 30 was the enemy, and the "hippies", as they came to be called, focused on protesting just about everything. Rock music became louder and more violent, marijuana and other drugs made their way into the mainstream scene (whereas before had been limited mostly to musicians), "free love" became a by-word—everybody was screwing everybody else, and there was a major event called "Woodstock" where thousands of hippies gathered in their tie-dyed clothing and smoked dope, made love, and listened to a parade of bands and singers. My career was in high gear and I had become part of the hippie culture although I was a few years older than most. Elaine and I were divorced, my father and I wrote a play together that was produced in Los Angeles and ran for several months, and right near the end of the decade I married Lynn and made my grand exit from Show-Biz.

The '70s, for me, was the Mother Earth decade. Richard Nixon was President until he was forced to resign for lying during the Watergate scandal, cocaine made its entry onto the drug scene, the rock music turned into Disco, and Lynn and I were divorced after she ran off with the Guru and her girl-friend. All in all, a decade wherein for me, the highs were high and the lows were the lowest. The "Cold War" with the Soviet Union and Communism was at its peak and everybody lived in fear of an impending nuclear war which, thank God, never happened.

The '80s were an amazing time. Suzie and I got married. Everybody with half a brain got rich and consumerism ruled. Money was no object, prices were sky high but then so were the interest rates you could get on your money, and another sub-culture came to be: The Baby Boomers. These were the now-grown-up children of World War II who had married and were raising families of their own, bringing about a stereotype called "Yuppies"—Young Urban Professionals of either sex or a couple where both husband and wife worked, drove flashy cars, bought only status-symbol products, ate take-out dinners, and raised their kids by several new methods, most interesting of which was the extent to which men got involved in taking care of their children. The music world was focused on "Punk Rock," and dance clubs flourished all over the land. Television now was almost all in color and *Dallas* was the big-deal show.

The 90s brought the "Me" generation—selfish youngsters who believed the world was their oyster and theirs alone. It was the dawn of the Technological Age—computers, cellular telephones, palm pilots and the like—and most of the progenitors of the companies which sprung up were very young guys in their 20s. Instant millionaires were born either through heading up a computer-type company or buying its stock. Microsoft came into being and it's founder, a twenty-something kid named Bill Gates, became one of the world's richest men. Their wasn't any single big war to speak of, although there were little wars popping up all over the world, and terrorism found its foothold. "Rap" music replaced traditional rock and roll as the music of the streets, and thanks to TV revenues professional athletes began making millions of dollars a year. There was an historical political scandal in the '90s—President Bill Clinton was caught having sex with a young intern—in the Oval Office, yet!—and was impeached by the House of Representatives for allegedly lying about it under oath. He was acquitted by the senate, however, much to the relief of most clear-thinking people, I among them. He may have been totally amoral, but he was the smartest man to hold that high office in my lifetime.

There were great fears around the end of the '90s that the upcoming change of millennia—the year 2000—was going to cause terrible havoc in the world of computers, which pretty much ran the world. Arguments raged over the future of "Y2K," basically over whether the computers would "recognize" the shift and react properly, and many feared disastrous results—air crashes, electrical failures, dead phones—all manner of Doomsday predictions were tossed into the ring, but as you well know, the entry into the second millennium was smooth as silk. The single biggest event of the 1990's? The birth of Hannah Michelle Lawrence in on June 8, 1998. I got the call on the tenth hole of the Rancho Park Golf Course about ten in the morning, and Suzie and I were in the hospital in Redwood City less than four hours later. Oh, that reminds me—after over 50 years of playing golf, I finally got a hole-in-one on Rancho's 16th hole in 1995.

Two miracles on the same golf course. How about that??

So far, this millennium is only two years old, but it has already brought us Sophie Alexandra Lawrence on August 15, 2000, and a new President in George W. Bush. The big event of this century so far would of course be "9/11"—that is the date when Arab terrorists flew hi-jacked airliners into the World Trade Center and the Pentagon, taking over 3000 lives and destroying the New York City's two giant landmark buildings. I wonder how many years will pass before people forget that date? Today, as I write this, it is December 7, 2002, 61 years since the bombing of Pearl

Harbor. There are a couple of national recognition ceremonies planned, but I haven't heard one person mention that today is "Pearl Harbor Day." Interesting, eh?   It's obviously too early to re-cap the '00s, so I'll just re-iterate what I said earlier—I hope they bring us interesting times.

The Beginning

I was born in New York City with a silver spoon in my mouth—literally.

My paternal grandfather, Maurice Rapp, was a silversmith in his native Austria, and although he became a tailor when he and his family were driven out of their homeland into England in 1901, he retained enough of his old talent to fashion a monogrammed spoon and cup upon my birthday—May 22, 1934.

By that time my father and his family had been in the United States since 1926, and by the time I was born Dad had already established himself as a comedy writer of some eminence. He was not yet the legendary Philip Rapp who created "The Bickersons" and "Baby Snooks" among his myriad credits, but he was on his way.

Dad got his comedy start in vaudeville, where he was the Rapp half of the eccentric-dance team of Morris and Rapp. Working on the same bills with the top comics of that day—George Burns, Bob Hope, Eddie Cantor, Milton Berle, Benny Rubin, The Marx Brothers, Jack Benny and lots of other people forgotten today but major stars in their time—he began selling jokes for whatever the traffic would bear. A dollar, two dollars—there was no offer too small. As Dad once told me when I began my own writing career and complained about a couple of very small offers: "Ideas are a dime a dozen. If somebody wants to buy something and you have no other offers, sell, and write something else."

It was in vaudeville that he met my mother, Mariam, who was also part of a dance act. It was what they called a "sister act," although my Mom's partner was not her sister. Not that my mother lacked for siblings—she was born in Chicago in 1911, the 12th child in a family of 12 children. (Funny story about that: Up until she was 65 we celebrated my

Dad and I on the Boardwalk in Palm Beach, 1935

mother's birthday on December 28th, right after Christmas. When she turned 65, Mom sent away for her birth certificate in order to collect her Social Security, and guess what? It turned out her *real* birthday was November 11th, which was known then as Armistice Day, a national holiday celebrating the end of World War I. With so many kids in the house, and my maternal grandparents being immigrants from Russia, Mom's birthday had not been duly noted by the family other than to remember it was right around some winter holiday. When she found out the date of her actual birthday, my mother delivered one of the funniest lines I have ever heard: "No wonder my life has been such a mess," she declared. "I've been reading the wrong horoscope for 65 years!")

My mother and father were married in 1931, and I know they had it very rough in those beginning years. It was the Depression, and salaries on the vaudeville circuit were minimal at best—*when* you had a booking. Dad liked to tell the story of how one time he and Mom bought a single potato and lived on potato soup for three days, cooked up by dipping the spud nightly into a pot of hot water! Of course, that wasn't the only soup they concocted—they were among the many thousands who took their meals at the Automat—ketchup mixed with boiling water to make a thin, but free, tomato soup.

Dad's fortunes began to rise when he found himself under the super-sized wing of a man named David Freedman, generally credited with inventing the sitcom as we know it today. (Or should that be "blamed"?) David, a huge, hulking man—6'5", somewhere north of 300 pounds—was much in demand in New York, writing sketches and jokes for all the top comics of the day, plus radio programs for some of those early days' personalities. He took on my 25-year-old father as his writing assistant in the very early 1930s, and it was under David' s tutelage that my father honed his craft. Among their many assignments, Dad and David wrote sketches for *The Ziegfeld Follies*, one of which was a skit for Fanny Brice which starred a little-girl character named Baby Snooks. This became the signature character for Fanny, who was later memorialized in the Barbra Streisand movies *Funny Girl* and *Funny Lady* and is still today recognized as one of the greatest comediennes of all time. "Snooks", to this day, is considered a classic radio sketch. Dad's co-creation of Baby Snooks sealed his legacy, but it was only just the beginning.

Dad used to tell some great stories about David, a real New York character. David's upper-east-side apartment was a literal joke factory. All day long comics were coming in the front door to pick up their "exclusive" material while others were ushered out the back lest they meet their hated rivals. The story I remember best about David exemplified his enormous "chutzpah": One night a sold-out heavyweight championship fight was scheduled at the old Madison Square Garden, and although he had no tickets, David assured my father they would both be at ringside for the bout. His plan was simple: My father was to walk up to one of the ticket-takers and boldly announce: "When Mr. Freedman arrives, please tell him Mr. Rapp is waiting at ringside." Before the ticket-taker could react, Dad was inside. A few minutes later, the huge, imposing figure of David Freedman loomed over the usher. "Is Mr. Rapp here yet?" he inquired. "Oh, yes sir, Mr. Freedman," said the usher. "He said you should meet him at ringside." And he did. That was David Freedman.

My father and David were writing the Eddie Cantor radio program in 1935 when Cantor was summoned to Hollywood, where he would make movies and broadcast his program from Tinseltown. Cantor wanted Dad and David to accompany him out West, but nothing could tempt David to leave his beloved New York, so Dad packed up the family—Mom, one-year-old me, and my wayward Uncle Johnny, Dad's youngest brother who was a class-cutting, pool-playing, brilliant 19-year-old and on his way to a life of delinquency—and loaded us aboard a ship which would take us through the Panama Canal to Hollywood.

Soon after we arrived in California we were ensconced in a Beverly Hills mansion, and assuming a pattern that was going to last the rest of his life, Dad strove daily to spend at least as much as he made. He bought a ranch in San Fernando Valley—3 acres with a house for Mom and him and another for my brother Paul and me—a stable with riding horses for everyone in the family, race horses, yachts, servants, Hillcrest Country Club, Cadillacs—if it was for sale, my Papa bought it! And his friends shared the wealth as well. If somebody suggested they go fishing—meaning buy a ticket on the half-day boat out of Santa Monica Pier—my father would be instantly on the phone ordering a private yacht replete with a Captain and a fully-stocked larder.

My brother and I lacked for nothing as children and teenagers—cars, clothes, golf-clubs, personalized bowling balls—so when the money ran out near the end of my parents' life, Paul and I were more than glad to support them. From the Beverly Hills manse they had descended to a tiny two-bedroom apartment, but it was still in Beverly Hills and they still retained the same telephone number they'd been assigned in 1935.

I remember one day that pretty much summed up Dad's rise and fall: He was sitting in his living room petting his beloved Puli, Ella, when he looked up at me wistfully and said, "Sad, isn't it? I made a fortune in my lifetime and all I saved up was a dog."

A couple of examples of Dad's profligacy:

He loved to have a local barber come by the house and shave him every morning. Talk about self-indulgence! But it made him feel like the

Paul, Mom, Dad and I, 1943

King he imagined himself to be. I remember the day when my Mother gave him bloody hell for this ridiculous expenditure. "Why can't you shave yourself like everybody else?" (Of course, the fact that she was having a massage in her bedroom while her dressmaker waited downstairs to give her a fitting took some of the sting out of her rebuke.)

Another time we were traveling to New York on the most expensive cross-country carrier of its time—the express train called the Super Chief. At dinner the first night out my father was overwhelmed by the food in the elegant dining car. He asked the maitre d' if he might see the Chef, and soon thereafter a huge black man wearing a toque appeared from the dining car kitchen. His name was David, and he almost fainted when my father looked at him and said: "David, how would you like to come to work for me in Beverly Hills? You'll be our cook and chauffeur, have your own room, and I'll double what you're making here on the train!" David took off his toque on the spot, my father put him up in the Waldorf Astoria during our New York stay, and David returned to Los Angeles with us as a passenger and was a trusted employee in our home for almost 10 years!

The beginning of the idea that my father was somebody "special" didn't come clear to me until a night in 1940 that I never shall forget. Dad and a bunch of his cronies were playing poker in our sumptuous living room, swearing and shouting while beclouded behind cigar and cigarette smoke. The whiskey was flowing and the chips were clattering until some-time after 2 in the morning when the party finally broke up and the last of the cronies stumbled out the door. I had awakened just before the festivi-ties ended and had been watching the gang from up at the top of the stairs, and when the final guest left, my mother and father got into a tremendous row. " I never want those bum friends of yours in this house again!" screamed my mother, and stormed out of the room.

It wasn't until a few years later that I found out those "bum friends" were Al Jolson, Cantor, Harpo Marx, Frank Morgan, and Berle!

THE BICKERSONS

For those of you unfamiliar with "The Bickersons," John and Blanche Bickerson were a married couple portrayed by Frances Langford and Don Ameche on the radio during the late 1930s and early 1940s. John Bickerson snored like a steamboat, and poor Blanche would be awakened in the middle of every night. She would start a "fight" with John—although my father insisted to his dying day that the Bickersons didn't fight, they sim-ply bickered. The truth is that the sketches were simply reportage of Mom and Dad's personal life. Almost every joke in the legendary sketches had actually been uttered sometime during one of the 63-years worth of nights they spent together.

Here's a sample of some Bickerson dialogue, overheard in the middle of the night of their eleventh wedding anniversary, shortly after Blanche has awakened a snoring, bleating John:

BLANCHE: John, we can't go on like this. We've been mar-
           ried eleven years and every year it gets worse.

JOHN: Oh boy…

BLANCHE: I'll never forget this anniversary as long as I live.
           You don't show up for the party, you don't get me
           a present—not even an anniversary card!

JOHN: I told you fifty times I got you a card!

BLANCHE: Well, where is it?

JOHN: It must have got lost in the mail.

BLANCHE: You're lying. Swear.

JOHN: I swear I'm lying.

BLANCHE: What?

JOHN: I mean I'm not lying. It was trimmed with lace
             and it had a wonderful poem on it. I picked it
             especially for you.

BLANCHE: What did it say on it?

JOHN: Go to sleep.

BLANCHE: If you picked it especially for me, I want to know
             what it said!

JOHN: It said, "Happy anniversary to my Love…"

BLANCHE: That could be anybody.

JOHN: Let me finish! It said, "Happy anniversary to my
             Love, my wife, my life, my turtle dove—life with
             you is great it seems, I love you more than pork
             and beans!"

BLANCHE: Very funny!

JOHN: Well how the hell do I know what it said? I can't
             remember the stupid poetry they put on those
             things!

BLANCHE: How can you behave like you do? And after I
             gave you the best years of my life.

JOHN: (*Sits up in bed and stares*) Were those the best?

BLANCHE: You needn't be sarcastic. I've tried to be a good
             wife to you.

JOHN: Okay, I admit it. You're the most tolerant wife in
             the world. (*He reaches down and takes a package
             from under his bed.*) And the truth is I DID buy
             you an anniversary present.

BLANCHE: You had it all the time!

JOHN: Yes, but I was too stupid and angry to give it to
             you. Happy anniversary, Blanche.

BLANCHE: You're sweet, John. I hope you didn't spend a lot
             of money.

JOHN: I didn't have a lot of money.

(Blanche opens the package and takes out an Auto-Bridge game.)

BLANCHE: This is beautiful. What is it?

JOHN: It's an auto-bridge game. Set me back eleven
                    dollars.

BLANCHE: Eleven dollars?? We've been married eleven years
                    and that's all I'm worth to you? Eleven dollars?

JOHN: Blanche…

BLANCHE: A dollar a year for cooking your meals, washing
                    your clothes, darning you socks, feeding your
                    children…

JOHN: We haven't got any children!

BLANCHE: Well what do you want for a dollar a year??!

And so it goes…

Getting the Bickersons on the air was not an easy task. My father conceived the idea as a seven-minute sketch while he was writing the *Maxwell House Coffee Time* with Fanny, Frank Morgan, and Carmen Dragon's orchestra. The year was 1938. Don Ameche was the announcer on the show and Frances Langford sang with Carmen's band. Dad wrote a sample sketch and took it to the all-powerful head of CBS, William Paley. Paley agreed it was funny, but forbade my father to broadcast it. "People do not want to listen to people fighting!' Dad argued in vain, but Paley would not be swayed. There would be no budget to hire actors to play John and Blanche and the skit would not go on the air.

Risking everything, Dad secretly cast Don and Frances as John and Blanche and literally snuck the sketch into a broadcast one Sunday afternoon. (In those days they used to do two shows—one for the east at 4 o'clock in the afternoon, and a second for the West Coast at 7.) The sketch was an enormous hit. The laughs were so loud and so many that the seven minutes stretched into 12, throwing the entire show off its timing and necessitating the cut of a Morgan sketch at the end.

When Paley heard the intro—"Ladies and Gentlemen, we now present Philip Rapp's creation, 'The Honeymoon is Over,' starring Don Ameche and Frances Langford as John and Blanche Bickerson."—he went into a rage and called the West Coast at once to inform Dad of his firing. But by the time the sketch was over, Paley was doubled up with laughter and was forced to admit Dad had been right. The Bickersons became a staple of several programs, and has endured to this day where it is played on many radio stations on a regular basis. In fact, the Battling Bickersons has become part of the language as a synonym for couples who tend not to get along. By the way—few people know that the extremely short life of Jackie Gleason's "Honeymooners" sketch was due to the fact my father sued Gleason for plagiarism, won the suit and got an injunction against them making any more shows.

Although he wrote dozens of radio shows, dozens of TV shows and dozens of movies, The Bickersons were my father's legacy. When we co-wrote a play starring John and Blanche, an hilarious show that played for months at the Coronet Theater in Los Angeles, Whitney Blake, who played Blanche, asked him one day if he really considered the Bickersons his legacy. "Wouldn't you rather depict a happier couple?" she asked. "There are no happy marriages," my father declared. "Marriage is for women. It's a disaster for men." "But a play needs heart," countered Whitney. "A woman needs heart!" responded Dad. "Not even a little bit of warmth?" she pleaded. "I will not yield to that. I hate warmth. I cannot stand it with every ounce of my being." And then my father explained for the thousandth time what the Bickersons were really all about:

"I don't consider that the Bickersons fight. It's all a result of frustration, confusion, and exhaustion. When I was married, my wife discovered that I snore terribly. She constantly woke me so that I'd stop. Now, when someone wakes me at 3 in the morning I'm not responsible for what I say. And since that time, the Bickersons has been sheer reporting, my wife writing half the lines. The point is, the Bickersons don't mean what they say either. When they argue, they aren't fighting. Life would be pretty dull without any arguments, anyway."

The proof of the pudding is that my parents were married for nearly 63 years, and when my mother passed away, my father's grief was heartbreaking to see.

Dad Fiddles While Mom Births...

My father was an inveterate gambler. Horses, mostly—but he was known to pay an occasional visit to one of the illegal gambling casinos operating quite openly on the Sunset Strip—on this particular night it was the gambling-room upstairs at Ciro's, a famous Hollywood nightspot.

It was the night of October 24, 1938. My mother was in the hospital, in labor with my brother-to-be, and the doctor had told Dad nothing would happen until at least morning, and most likely Mom would have to have a C-section if there was no baby by noon. So Dad decided to go gambling. After only a couple of hours at the famed nightclub/casino, Diamond Jim Rapp had lost 25 thousand dollars—which he paid for with a check—from an account in which he had no money!

Imagine his predicament—first and foremost, how would he ever explain such a tremendous loss to my mother, especially while she was struggling to have his kid—and how was he going to cover that check by morning?

Ever resourceful and refusing to panic, my father dashed home and sat down at his typewriter. He'd had an idea for a screenplay for several weeks and had done nothing about it, but by eight o'clock in the morning he had finished a 30-page treatment! He called the hospital and learned that they would have to do a C-section after all and it was scheduled for noon. He'd best be at the hospital by eleven. The clock was ticking.

He showered and shaved and then he picked up the phone and called Harry Cohn at Columbia Pictures. Cohn was head of the studio and one of the most hated men in Hollywood. (When he died, hundreds of people turned out for his funeral. An actor who had a particularly sour relationship with Cohn remarked, "Give the people something they want and they'll show up in droves.") For whatever reason, however, my father and Harry got along just fine. Cohn agreed to see him at noon, but my father insisted it be no later than ten. He had a story he wanted Harry to read and he needed an answer right away.

Me and Mom, 1936

So Dad showed up at the Gower Street Studio at ten o'clock and by five-after Harry Cohn was locked up in his office reading the treatment while Dad paced nervously in the outer office, preparatory to pacing nervously in the waiting room at Cedars. Fifteen minutes later, Cohn buzzed for my father to come in. "Okay," said Harry. "I'll buy it. Twenty-five G's, take it or leave it." My father fought back a grin of triumph. "Well…okay. But I want a check right now." At this point Cohn got a little miffed. What the hell was the big hurry? My father, having really no choice, told Harry the truth—he'd lost a bundle gambling and needed the money to cover a check before my

Bathing beauty Mom

mother found out. Basically sympathetic, Cohn had the check cut and my father made it to the bank and the hospital in plenty of time to welcome Paul Winston Rapp.

My father had committed the perfect crime. Almost. A couple of weeks later, while Dad was out somewhere and my mother was still recuperating in bed from the surgery, she answered the telephone and found herself speaking to a man named Jack Hellman, who was one of the top writers at the show-business bible, *Variety*. "What's up with that picture Phil sold to Columbia?" Jack asked. "What picture?" was my mother's reply, and Jack proceeded to spill the entire can of beans. I was only four years old, but I think I recall Mom waiting at the front door with a baseball bat when Dad came home.

It all worked out, however. Mom forgave him when he convinced her there'd been no blood—he'd have never written that screen treatment if he hadn't gambled away the money, so nothing really was lost when you thought about it. For whatever reason, my mother decided to buy that somewhat flawed logic, and as for the picture, it never got made. My father always suspected that Cohn's purchase was a "mercy buy," but whatever it was, it bailed him out of a tough one and for that he was forever grateful.

V-J Day In Hollywood

Certain events occur in our lifetimes that are so significant we never forget where we were when we first heard the news; the bombing of Pearl Harbor, JFK's assassination, RFK's murder, the night they caught O.J…(Poppy's note to H. & S.—O.J. Simpson was a truly great football star who was accused of murdering his wife and another young man. His trial took a year and was televised across the country and it was clear to almost everybody that he was guilty as sin. But his attorneys played what they called "The Race Card"—The LAPD was notorious for framing black men, and this, his lawyer's claimed, was just such a case. Given that almost everyone on the jury was black, the defense's ploy worked and O.J. was acquitted. He was later convicted in a civil trial. Sorry, anyone else, but I told you I was writing this for Hannah and Sophie to read down the road.)

Where was I? Oh, yes. I was 7 years-old when I heard the announcement of the Japanese bombing of Pearl Harbor come over the big, stand-up Atwater-Kent radio in the living room of our ranch in Encino. I'll never forget that radio, either. It was top-of-the-line for it's day—about four-feet tall, made out of shiny wood with tallish carved legs and a big wooden cut-out figure of a stag leaping across the speaker. It was a Sunday morning, and I was still in my pajamas reading the comics while my mother and father traded other parts of the paper. When the news came about the surprise attack, my mother and father bolted upright and went stone silent as President Roosevelt intoned the news of the "day that will live in infamy." I didn't really comprehend much other than the "Japs", which we were now licensed to call them, had perpetrated a sneak attack on our ships in Hawaii and it would mostly likely mean we were going to war with Japan. And, as I remember my parents predicting, at last declaring war against Germany

21

and getting into that fray. Actually, to a 7-year-old kid it was all sort of exciting, and I remember the war years vividly. There was lots of rationing of gasoline, foodstuffs, and other essentials. We grew a victory garden out at the ranch, my father bought a couple of pigs, a bunch of chickens, and built a smoke house so we never had to lack for eggs or bacon during the years when things like that were severely rationed. We saved paper, and tin foil, and rubber bands, and bought War Stamps and War Bonds—and many of my father's friends marched off to war. (My father was 4-F due to a blood condition but contributed greatly writing sketches for various government entertainment programs and films.)

There was lots of propaganda dispensed during the war years. Caricatures of Tojo and Hitler were everywhere to be found in comic books, magazines, billboards, movie theaters—always depicting the Nazis and Japs as the most evil of villains, which they were, and always depicting Uncle Sam or a G.I. kicking them in the pants or somesuch. Patriotism was the order of the day in Hollywood—stars of both genders made trips to entertain the troops, gave their time to serve coffee and doughnuts at the Hollywood Canteen (all servicemen welcome for free) and dance with the young, homesick men.

The end of the war with Japan came after almost 4 years of intense fighting in the Pacific where hundreds of thousands of soldiers gave their lives. Far off islands like Bataan, Corregidor, Midway, and Iwo Jima became the subjects of every-day discussion. In August of 1945, shortly after we dropped two Atomic bombs on the Japanese homeland, the conflict ended. It was the first time the world had ever seen a nuclear weapon, and the mass destruction which the bombs wrought on Hiroshima and Nagasaki was indescribable. Japan surrendered almost at once, and almost at once the debate began—should we or should we not have unleashed this sort of weapon on innocent civilians no matter how many American military lives it might have saved in the long run. It was the dawn of the Nuclear Age.

The day the Japanese officially surrendered, called "V-J Day," August 14, 1945, I was at The Hitching Post Theater, a fabulous movie house on Hollywood Boulevard, just east of Vine Street. It showed only Western movies, and on the weekend they had a special Saturday Matinee Show. It usually consisted of a double-feature starring the likes of Hopalong Cassidy, or Gene Autry, or Roy Rogers; a couple of shorts, a chapter of a serial, a cartoon, and coming attractions—all for a quarter. The gimmick at the Hitching Post was that all the kids wore Western clothes, although that was not compulsory, but it *was* compulsory to check your six-shooter at the door. On a given Saturday afternoon one would find 500 be-chapped and be-spurred kids in the theater and a couple of hundred cap-pistols stored in the office.

On this particular summer afternoon I had arranged to meet my friend Johnny Cookson at the Hitching Post. Instead of taking the Red Car (a trolley line of red "streetcars" which ran from the beach to Down-town) I decided to ride my bike instead. I almost always took the streetcar which only cost ten cents to go anywhere on the line, but this was a beautiful day and it really wasn't a very difficult bike ride. So there I was, be-chapped and unarmed, sitting with Cookson watching a movie when suddenly we heard this tremendous commotion outside the theater.

Before the gathered kids could panic, the picture suddenly stopped, the lights came up, and an usher came running out onto the stage, shout-ing "The war is over, the war is over, the Japs have surrendered…" Out-side the noise was growing ever louder. Johnny and I whooped it up in-side the theater along with everybody else who understood what a great day this was, and then finally made our way outside.

The scene on Hollywood Boulevard was surreal. A mob had formed in the middle of the street and the celebrants had tipped over a streetcar which was lying on its side in the middle of the street. (We later found out that the car had been evacuated before the mob turned it over.) Hundreds of people were running up and down the Boulevard, cars were stopped in their tracks blaring their horns in both joy and impatience, and to say the least it was wild and wooly out there.

Usually, after a movie, we'd go down to C.C. Brown's next door to the Grauman's Chinese theater and have a hot-fudge sundae but today we de-cided discretion was the better part of valor and we'd best be getting on home.

It was a lucky quirk of fate that I had ridden my bike that day. If I'd had to wait for a red car I'd probably still be standing out on Hollywood and Vine.

And you know what I just remembered? I never retrieved my gun that day. Just as well. I'm against guns.

An Eddie Cantor Vignette

Eddie Cantor was my Godfather, probably because he had a wife and five daughters and needed some kind of boy in the family. At any rate, almost as soon the boat bearing the Rapps and the Cantors arrived in L.A., Dad went to work on the radio show he'd been writing in New York with David Freedman. The master at last, Dad put Uncle Johnny to work as *his* apprentice, and the two of them began churning out the weekly half-hour scripts.

Dad was making a fortune for those times—any time, in fact: Seventy-five-hundred dollars a week—and no taxes! What he gave to Uncle Johnny remains a family secret, but Uncle Johnny didn't have to wait long to hit the big-time himself. Upon returning from Italy where he served in Special Forces, he went to work for Bob Hope and there he stayed for 17-years until his most untimely death at the age of 53.

Forgive me, but I must digress for a minute for a word or two about my favorite Uncle. John Rapp was one of the funniest people I ever knew; we were far more like friends than relatives. Unk loved to go gambling—Vegas, the track, the poker clubs—and I was cut from the very same cloth. His wife Blanche (get the connection—John and Blanche?) did not approve of this habit, so he had to invent cons to keep her from finding out. On more than one occasion Johnny and I told Blanche we were going fishing, only to fly up to Vegas for three or four hours and then return home, but not before stopping at a fish market to buy our "catch" and stink up our clothes. Despite his mammoth weekly paycheck from Hope, Johnny was perennially broke because Blanche kept him on a strict allowance which she doled out every Monday morning. By Wednesday he'd be cadging twenties here and there, but to his everlasting credit he always paid everybody back come allowance day.

Anyhow, about Cantor. Contrary to popular belief, Eddie was a son-of-a-bitch. The nice guy image was strictly an act. In private he could be downright mean, and sometime in 1937 my father and Uncle Johnny ran out of patience and walked away from the show, which due to Cantor's bent for changing jokes and altering sketches, was beginning to slip badly in the ratings.

A friend of Dad's and Johnny's summed up the entire Cantor walk-out with an hilarious gag: He had a phony copy of *Variety*, the show business bible, printed up and the headline read:

RAPPS DESERT SINKING SHIT!

Fanny Brice

One of my father's legendary accomplishments was the creation of Baby Snooks. Dad and his mentor, David Freedman, had been hired to write sketches for the Ziegfield Follies starring Fanny Brice, among others. They had an idea for a sketch which would feature Fanny as a little girl whose clarion call was "Why, daddy??" which drove her father to distraction.

The sketch was a tremendous success, my father's relationship with Fanny blossomed, and several years later, when she and Snooks got the call to become part of a national radio program, my father, who by now was firmly established in Hollywood, was tapped to write the show. The show was broadcast on a Thursday, and I remember that he used to hole himself up in his office on Wednesday nights and go to work. Thursday morning we'd wake up to find a script in a manila envelope waiting to be picked up by an NBC courier, and dad sawing wood in his bedroom. It has always amazed me that in these days when it takes dozens of writers to churn out a weekly half-hour show, Dad wrote these programs all by himself.

Although Fanny was officially my Godmother, I have few recollections of her myself. I *do* remember making several trips to the radio station to sit in the booth and watch as my father directed the show. Despite the fact it was merely a radio broadcast, Fanny always appeared as Snooks in a short, puffy little skirt, white socks and Mary-Janes, and a big bow in her hair. And I am reminded of her daily when I enter my living where a portrait of six-year-old me by the famous Hollywood painter, John Decker, commissioned by Fanny as a gift to my parents, hangs, but my visits to her home are merely dim memories. Dad, however, had dozens of stories about Fanny. The one that sticks out in my mind concerns the day she told Dad she was planning to wed Billy Rose, a shady character who was something of an entrepreneur. Fanny

FANNIE BRICE'S SECRET OF HOW TO KEEP SMILING

Radio Stars

JUNE
10
CENTS

THE LARGEST CIRCULATION OF ANY RADIO MAGAZINE

THE
CANDID PICTURE
MAGAZINE
OF RADIO

COMPLETE
COAST-TO-COAST
PROGRAM LISTINGS

FANNIE
BRICE

Fanny Brice as Baby Snooks

had only recently been divorced from Nicky Arnstein, a notorious gangster, and Billy was getting a divorce from the champion swimmer, Eleanor Holm,. Billy, among other ventures, owned the famed New York nightspot, The Stork Club, and most of his friends were mobsters. His temper was legendary, and even though he was a very little guy—he stood only about 5 ft. 3 in.—you didn't want to get on his bad side.

When Fanny gave Dad the news of her engagement to the diminutive little hoodlum, he was appalled. "You must be nuts!" he told her. "You just got a divorce from one gangster and now you're going to hook up with another one??"

"Well," said Fanny, somewhat sheepishly, "I couldn't quit cold turkey so I decided just to cut down."

The relationship between Dad and Fanny blew up in the early '40s when Dad decided he wanted his credit to precede Fanny's on the radio show: "It's Maxwell House Coffee Time, written and directed by Philip Rapp and starring Fanny Brice" was the way he wanted it. "It's my way or the highway," said Pop.

Fanny wouldn't give in, and my father made good his threat. The show continued on for several more years, however, with some top radio writers at the helm, and although they parted company with some acrimony, dad and Fanny later patched things up and were friends until the day she died.

Spring In Brazil

Although my father's résumé in littered top to bottom with hits, honest reporting forces me to reveal that he was also the author—literally—of what might arguably be the biggest flop, dollar for dollar, in the history of The Great White Way.

In 1945 my father conceived and wrote the book for a musical show called *Spring in Brazil*. It was a wonderful script—funny, colorful, lively—and it wasn't long before it found a producer. Actually, an *uber*-producer—Lee Shubert, of the famous Shubert Broadway dynasty. Mr. Lee's first act was to sign my father on as the director and next he engaged the songwriting team of Robert Wright and George Forrest, whose numerous Broadway credits included the score of the award-winning musical drama, *The Song of Norway*, the story of famed Norse composer Edvard Grieg. His next move was to cast Milton Berle and Rose Marie (of *The Dick Van Dyke Show* fame); then he went about the business of raising the money.

To say this was a mammoth production would be an understatement - the show had a cast of 32 speaking parts, 18 singers (one of whom was Jack Cassidy who went on to stardom and marriage to Shirley Jones), and 27 dancers—not to mention a dance director, costume designers, a musical director, a chorale director and an orchestrator. The sum total to mount this production—and remember, we're talking 1945 dollars now—was somewhere close to $800,000! I don't know exactly how much that translates to in today's dollars, but three million would probably be a safe enough guess.

After several weeks of strenuous rehearsal in New York, much of which I sat through since I'd come with my dad to New York during my summer vacation from school, the show was pronounced ready by all concerned and moved on to its initial booking: a two-week run in Chicago, to be followed by a similar stay in Boston and then, hopefully, a triumphal trip to Broadway where it would run for years and years.

31

SHUBERT Theatre

BOSTON

UNDER THE MANAGEMENT OF

MESSRS. LEE & J. J. SHUBERT

A big problem arose opening night in Chicago, however. Berle, who, through endless rehearsals, had become quite good in his role of "Walter Gribble, Jr.," lost his confidence in the character, the show, and his own abilities and threw away the book almost entirely. "Uncle Miltie" reverted to all his vaudeville Berleisms to get his laughs, so, needless to say, the evening was a disaster and the next day the critics panned the hell out of the show. The unkindest cut of all was the almost unanimous declaration that "if it weren't for Berle and his hysterical antics, the evening would have been a big, splashy waste."

My father and Mr. Lee were livid—they'd been warned that hiring Berle could prove to be a mistake; several insiders predicted that the comic's insecurities would pop up at the moment of truth and he'd ruin everything. It was obviously too late to recast the part, but Mr. Lee and my father raked Berle over the coals and warned him that if something like that should happen again, they'd close the show before it got to New York. Berle, of course, promised to behave.

The rest of the run in Chicago went fine and Berle performed the play as it was written. Unfortunately, the critics had already spoken and advance sales in New York were suffering accordingly.

Believe it or not, the night the show opened in Boston, Berle did it again! The turned-in feet, the lispy voice, the endless ad-libs once again destroyed the production and true to their word, Mr. Lee and my father closed the show that very night, not even waiting for what they knew would be vicious reviews and negligible advances in New York.

It was truly a tragic event, given all the money and work that went into that glorious production which I personally promise you was an absolute joy when properly performed.

My father and Berle hardly spoke over the next forty years, although both were members of Hillcrest Country Club and saw each other on a regular basis. I played golf with Milton one day, and during the round, the now much-subdued comic told me he'd always felt very badly about the fate of the show, and asked me to pass along his apologies to my father. I told him it would be better coming from him directly, but unfortunately it never did.

We all remember Milton Berle as "Mr. Television," but take it from me—"Mr. Broadway" he ain't!

May I Please Respin The Bottle?

I was somewhere around ten years old.

Some of us boys and girls from the neighborhood were having a party at Bunky Bernheim's house when somebody suggested we play a few of rounds of "Spin the Bottle." Being only ten, (all the other kids were the usual two years older) and attending an all-boys school, I didn't have a clue what kind of game that was, but what the heck, all the other kids were up for it so I went along with the flow.

When I saw what was involved I panicked. There was no way I was gonna kiss a girl! Absolutely not! But before I knew it, a little dark-haired girl who lived on the corner of Elm and Elevado had spun the bottle and it had wound up pointing at me.

No, I begged. Please, don't make me kiss her! But Bunky and my other "pals" were unrelenting. The bottle had pointed at me and I was obligated to kiss that little girl. So they literally held me down and beckoned the girl to come and give me a kiss She smiled and crawled across the circle on her hands and knees, and although I tried to turn my head away she managed to plant a really good smacker right on my lips! I almost died of embarrassment.

I'll never forget that night, ever. I wonder if Elizabeth Taylor remembers it, too?

School Days

I began my academic life like any other normal rich Beverly Hills kid—starting at age four, I was enrolled at the posh Mrs. Buckley's preschool in Brentwood where I must admit I excelled in both nursery school and kindergarten.

When it came time to move on to elementary school, my parents decided to send me to the hoity-toity Black-Foxe Military Institute, an expensive private academy located on Melrose and Wilcox in mid-Hollywood which had high marks for academics and was populated by lots of celebrity sons. I was six years old but very advanced scholastically for my age—Mrs. Buckley and my parents put great emphasis on academics— so I could actually read fluently by the time I left kindergarten. It was expected that I would be enrolled in the first grade, but back in those days, especially in private schools, kids were tested and advanced willy-nilly, irrespective of age, so when the folks at Black-Foxe tested me, they determined I was ready to begin my "higher education" in the fourth grade. Six-years-old in the fourth grade! Go figure.

Needless to say I was the smallest cadet in my class of eight students, one of whom was Mary Martin's son, Larry Hagman, who went on to TV stardom in shows such as *I Dream of Jeannie* and as JR on that seminal soap opera, *Dallas*. At first, I hated the school and all that it stood for— uniforms every day, marching drills with fake rifles during the hours when regular kids at regular schools were having recess—but with my mother and father's gentle urging to stick it out it didn't take long for me to accept my fate. I managed to get the highest grades in my class the first year, and was doing very well on the drill field where I was promoted to cadet corporal despite my diminutive size and young age. I finished the year with a gold medal for scholarship and a good-conduct medal to boot. Things weren't as bad as I had originally imagined.

Cadet Corporal Rapp, 1943

By the second year, however, the rigors of the daily drilling began to take their toll. The rifles were heavy, and the Southern California sun was inevitably at its peak during drill period. Marching around for an hour with the rifle on my shoulder and the sun beating down was getting me down. All of this drilling had a purpose, of course. Besides providing discipline, it prepared the cadet corps for the regular Friday Parades, wherein the parents showed up in droves to watch us parade around in our dress uniforms while the fabulous Black-Foxe band marched with us, playing Souza marches with amazing aplomb.

One day, when the temperatures had soared up over the hundred degree mark and we were out marching around as usual, it occurred to me that the band was no-where in sight. A little inquiring revealed that with the exception of the Friday parades, the band rehearsed during drill period—in a large, comfortable air-conditioned hall. Ah, I thought, that sounds like the way to go!

Next day I went over to the band hall and faced the band instructor, one Captain Milton Lockhart. I was, at that time, all of seven years old, and maybe 4 feet tall at the outside, but I had, as my father used to say, "the guts of a policeman." "I'd like to be in the band," I told Capt. Lockhart. "Oh?" he said, looking down and fighting back a smile. "And what instrument do you play?" "What instrument do you need?" was my rejoinder. "Well," he said, "I could use another trumpet player..." "Ah," I said, "what luck. The trumpet is my very favorite instrument!" Of course I had never lifted a trumpet in my life, and of course Capt. L. knew it, but he could see that I was a game little guy and he really did need another trumpet player, so to my everlasting gratitude, he said okay. By the end of the week I was transferred to the band and my marching days, with the exception of Friday parades, were over.

Actually, I became a pretty damn good trumpet player over the next three years. Harry James was my idol and I used to listen to his records and then play back his solos which sounded, to me, almost flawless. By eighth grade, my last year at BF, I had risen to the position of second trumpet and had begun to envision a career as an orchestra-leading trumpet player somewhere down the road.

Perhaps the highlight of my Black-Foxe trumpet playing career, other than joining two other trumpeters in a performance of a piece-for-horns called "The Three Kings" in a major Southern California band concert, came on the day that Franklin D. Roosevelt passed away.

Every day at school there was a "bugler-of-the-day", whose job it was to stand on a huge platform near the drill field and blow various bugle calls to signal the end of one class, a three-minute warning call, and a final call signifying every cadet should be settled in his next class. The day FDR died I was bugler of the day, and it fell to me to play Taps as the entire corps lined up in mourning on the drill field. Needless to say I was a nervous wreck, but I played that bugle call as it has never been played before. I can still see myself standing on that podium, 500 blue-uniformed cadets standing before me with rifles raised in a military salute, and the sad tones of my trumpet echoing over the field. It made that long ago visit to Captain Lockhart all worthwhile.

How did my trumpet playing career play out? Well, I pretty much abandoned it once I got to high school since it no longer served the purpose of excusing me from drill. But my beautiful silver and gold Olds horn certainly came in handy during my wild and wooly young adult years: Several times, when down to my last few pennies, I took it to the local pawn shop and hocked it for the rent. After five or six pawnings, however, I finally decided the old fellow had served its purpose and simply left it in hock.

Rest in peace, old friend, wherever you may be.

I entered Beverly Hills High School in September of 1945 at the ripe old age of 11. Needless to say I was the youngest student there, and I was also the smallest, having not yet reached a height of five-feet. My parents and the administration were somewhat worried as to whether or not I could fit in with the other ninth-graders, but for whatever reason I had no problem whatsoever.

I applied for and won the job as water-boy for the football team, which gave me a close, personal relationship with that creme-de-la-creme of all high school students, the football jocks; the gorgeous gang of pom-pom girls thought I was just the cutest little thing ever and treated me as such and with the exception of algebra I was able to make very good grades.

Not much unusual happened during my high-school days. I became very interested in journalism and decided I would become a sports-writer some day. I furthered that ambition somewhat by becoming Sports Editor of the school paper, Highlights, and held a similar position during my senior year at the yearbook, The Watchtower. I continued to do well scholastically (with the exception of math and science courses where I was quite properly considered to be a basket case), I sprouted up to a height of nearly five-foot ten, but when it came near time to graduate in June of 1949 my folks and I did a little re-considering.

We agreed that at 15 I was a tad too young to be moving on to college, so with the blessings of the school administration, I stayed on at Beverly for an extra year. It was a rather easy nine-month exercise — classes in stage-crew, print shop, phys-ed and similar non-taxing subjects comprised my curriculum, until finally, in June of 1950, I marched across the stage and took my diploma.

I'm proud to say I was voted two honors by my fellow graduates: Quickest Wit and Most Loquacious. That means I talked a lot.

Not bad for a just-16-year-old kid if I do say so myself.

FIGHT ON FOR OLD SC

I was accepted at Yale, Missouri, and the University of Southern California, the three schools to which I had applied, since all three had exceptional journalism courses. After much

JOEL RAPP
BEVERLY HILLS H. S.
50TH YEAR REUNION

The Portrait of Dorian Rapp

consideration, I decided to stick close to home and enrolled at USC.

Located in the heart of south-central Los Angeles, USC has a beautiful campus, and although I joined a fraternity—Zeta Beta Tau—I chose to live at home with my parents my first year in school. I think it was a wise decision, as I wasn't quite ready to move into a house with a bunch of 19 and 20-year-olds, and the daily commute was less than half and hour.

My freshman year was basically without incident. I made lots of friends in the fraternity and maintained a B+ grade average, the only blips being a hard-fought C in a required science class. Journalism class was basic but professional and I began dating a lovely girl from Beverly Hills High, my first real experience with the opposite sex. Lots of guys in the fraternity were dating high-school girls at that time, so I was not embarrassed by this act of "robbing the cradle". After all, I was still basically in the cradle myself.

Right before the beginning of my sophomore year, by which time I had moved into the fraternity house, (but I still took my laundry home every weekend) the school announced the beginning of a new major: Telecommunications. By that time I had begun to have second thoughts about a career in journalism, having found out the basic pay rates for said

College frat dance. Left front, Judy W., my very first love.

profession and greedily hungering for more. I decided to switch majors—basically, I told my faculty advisor, I wanted to go into my father's business: I would become a writer of TV and movies.

Television was still an infant medium in 1952, and the equipment in our department was crude at best. The teachers, too, were just getting their own feet wet, but the various classes in writing and production were valuable experiences. I'll never forget one production class taught my a young man named Ed DeRoo. Our class assignment was to produce a 10-minute live documentary program, and I chose to re-create an operation. I contacted a friend of my father's, Dr. Leon Belous, and eagerly accepted an invitation to join him and his surgical team in the operating room to observe a hysterectomy. I was amazed at the cavalier attitude of the surgeons as they dug around in this woman's open stomach, discussing the upcoming weekend's football games and other such mundane subjects as they mucked around in the poor woman's pulsating innards.. The operation was a complete success, however, and I managed to translate it almost perfectly when it came time for me to show-case my production.

As proud as I was of my work, Mr. DeRoo was not as complimentary. He gave me a B, and when I complained that I thought my production was far and away the best in the class, he agreed, but said he gave me a B because in his opinion I didn't put forth my best effort. Perplexed, I took my B and slunk off to my next semester, but not many years later I got a chance to get even. I was producing and directing a very, very low budget movie called "High School Big Shot" (which I had also written) when who should come in auditioning for a part but Ed DeRoo himself. He was properly surprised and respectful to find his former student in a position of such eminence, and he gave an excellent reading for the part. When he was done, I shook my head sadly. "I'm sorry, Ed," I intoned. "You did very well, but I don't think it was your best work." I thought he was going to cry, until I grinned and told him he had the job. Ah, revenge is sweet.

My college career was not without its highlights. I became a member of the Trojan Squires, the underclass men's honor organization, during my sophomore year, and a member of the Trojan Knights during my junior and senior semesters; I won the office of President of the College of Letters, Arts and Sciences in my senior year, and just narrowly lost the vote for President of my fraternity.

The most memorable and significant event of my college career oc-

Nancy C., my college sweetheart

curred in 1954: There was a secret fraternity on the SC campus called Theta Nu Epsilon, or TNE, or colloquially, The Tong. You may have heard of it as the Skull and Bones. Some of its more famous alumni include Richard Nixon associates John Erlichman and Tom Haldeman. This organization, banned by congressional decree, operated secretly on many campuses in the U.S., and its main purpose was to control student body elections. It's membership was composed of two members each from about 75% of the fraternities on campus, and it was a foregone conclusion that the people TNE backed for school offices were shoo-ins to win.

This was vitally important, since the more student officers and jocks that a fraternity could boast meant the choice of the best potential pledges. Each year new TNE members were selected by the graduating seniors from the respective houses, and at the end of my junior year I was informed by our senior representative that I would be his replacement the following year.

I was thrilled. Even though you could be expelled from school if it were discovered you were a member of this underground organization, the idea of representing my fraternity and helping select high student body officials more than made up for the risks.

Everything I had heard whispered about TNE turned out to be true. The meetings were held once a week in secret locations, and all the members wore black cloaks and hoods, similar to the outfits worn by the Ku Klux Klan. There was a giant skull that was placed on the table and over pitchers of beer, debates were held to select the various candidates.

Things were going along just dandy, until one fateful evening our TNE meeting was uncovered by a young man who had ambitions to swim against the tide and run for Student Body President without our support. Before we could negotiate a deal to back him in his attempt, thus avoiding a nasty confrontation, he had reported us to the Dean of Students and trouble was on its way.

I remember it like it was yesterday. I was summoned to the office of the Dean of Men, and I was positive my days at USC were over. When I reached the office I decided to tell the truth and throw myself on the mercy of Dean Hyinck.

Yes, I told him there *is* a TNE. Yes, I am the President, and yes, we do select the people who hold high student office. But here I was, a Trojan Knight, about to graduate *cum laude*, so I begged him for a reprieve. He considered my case for a couple of days,, and then called me at the frat house and told me that if we would disband the Tong and I would bring in the robes, the skulls and all the other TNE accouterments, he'd let me off the hook. I instantly acquiesced.

The next day I appeared in his office with a trunkful of illicit stuff. Reporters and photographers from our school newspaper, *The Daily Trojan*, were on hand to record the event, and the next day it was front page news. Pictures of me handing over the skull to the Dean took up practically all the space above the fold, followed by a story revealing that I had vowed the organization had been disbanded and would never appear on campus again.

Yeah, right!

The next week, at our regular meeting, we produced a second set of robes and a substitute skull and went on about our usual business of selecting a slate of candidates for the upcoming election. You can be sure that from that day forward we were much, much more careful about where and when we convened.

A few months later I graduated with my Class.

I do not know whether TNE still flourishes on the SC campus.

And I wouldn't tell you if I did.

I Will Go To Korea! (Not!)

A terrifying thing happened to me during the height of the Korean War. I was almost drafted!

For those of you who don't remember the Korean War, it followed World War II, which followed World War I, ("The War to End All Wars") and preceded the Vietnam War which preceded the Gulf War; and all but one of these wars was fought during a period during which we were engaged 24/7 in a Cold War with the USSR. There have been several little wars since then all over the globe, and as I write these words (in 2002) we are about to go to war with Iraq. Apparently there are lots of people who don't buy the words of the Civil War's General Sherman who declared, "War is hell."

About Korea: Soon after the end of World War II, around 1950, the world was teetering on the brink of falling into Communist hands. The Asian country of Korea was divided into two sections—North Korea, which was controlled by the Communists, and South Korea, which was not. The United States and other countries of the so-called Free World decided that the Communists must be driven out of North Korea lest all of Asia fall to the evil Reds—and the saviors would be young men between the ages of 18 and 30. (I'm sure you've noticed that all wars are started by old men who then send young men out to fight them.)

The draft was still in effect in the early 1950s, but I was in college when the Police Action in Korea became a full-fledged war and thus I was deferred from military service. Actually, I wasn't really worried about being drafted since I had a heart condition called *paroxysmal tachychardia* which translated means that under certain stressful physical situations my heart would go off and begin pounding a hundred miles an hour—actually, about 160 beats a minute versus the normal 60 or so—and when I got such an attack I literally had to lie down and wait for the palpitations to stop, which was sometimes as long as 15 minutes. Several letters from prominent cardiologists confirmed this condition, along with a description of my lifelong hypertension, so I was pretty sure I'd be classified 4-F when my draft number came up. I mean if a guy with flat feet could be 4-F...

Sometime during my senior year at USC I was called by the Selective Service Board for a pre-induction physical—a physical which was given to every male with a draft card months, sometimes years, prior to his actual induction. I went to that physical and to my amazement, despite my plethora of doctors' notes, I was classified 1-A. Obviously the members of my local draft board were not impressed by my letters so I prepared myself for the worst. Not that I'm not a patriot, but my years of practicing Orthodox Cowardice told me I wouldn't like winding up in the infantry, dodging enemy bullets, not to mention suffering the two-year halt to my rising career and social life.

The worst came soon after I graduated and could garner no more deferments lest I go to graduate school, which, frankly, was never an option. Within about a year I got the fateful letter from the President of the United States, Dwight D. Eisenhower himself, greeting me and informing me that I should report for induction into the Army on such and such a date. Eisenhower had gotten elected on the promise that "I will go to Korea," and everybody presumed that meant he would go over there, talk to their honchos, and stop the war ASAP. The war did eventually end during his term, but too late for my sorry butt. This whole army thing could not have come at a worse time in my life: I was already working as a second-assistant director, I had a pretty cool apartment in Brentwood (very near where O.J. did his alleged thing), a nice new car and a bevy of excellent girl-friends. But all was not lost. Through a contact of my father's, I sent a letter to the Commander of Fort Dix in New Jersey which was a special service unit that made various military-themed films. I asked if there was a way I could wangle a transfer to that base given my show-biz experience, and the Commander responded rather quickly that as soon as I finished my basic training my request would be fulfilled. It was a big load off my mind, because I didn't want to be the first Beverly Hills Jew to carry a gun in warfare.

(My Uncle Johnny was drafted during World War II, and he was scared silly and totally unsuited for the whole military thing: During Basic Training he paid some guy to take care of his foot-locker, clean his rifle, whatever.

Meanwhile, my father was frantically pulling strings with his Washington D.C. contacts trying to find some sort of cushy assignment for his brother, and just before Johnny graduated from basic the news came that thanks to my father's relentless string-pulling he was going to be attached to a Special Services Unit. Imagine the family celebration upon learning the news—until we found out what the posting was going to be: Johnny was being sent to Italy, where from the "safety" of a truck he would be playing records for our troops in the trenches, who were returning gunfire from the Axis troops across the way. Johnny would broadcast several hours of the day from a strategically placed discmobile with loudspeakers on top (remember Robin Williams in *Good Morning, Vietnam*? That was Johnny in WWII!) Thanks to my father's tireless efforts, Uncle Johnny had wound up a sitting duck. Luckily, he escaped unscathed and came back to a hugely successful writing career with the legendary Bob Hope.)

My induction date approached, and I went about the tasks of giving up my apartment, selling my car, and saying goodbye to each of my girl-friends on consecutive nights. For 48 hours before the morning I was to report, I partied. Drinking, smoking, not sleeping, swallowing dexedrine tablets, drinking coffee—I figured what the hell, I was going away for two years so why not go out with a bang. Maybe my heart would blow up and I could avoid the inconvenience of the Army that way.

On December 27, 1955, my father drove me to the Induction Center in downtown L.A. and we said our sad goodbyes. In I went, scared shitless, and joined the mob of other equally scared young men for Phase One of the process: The mental test (the test Muhammad Ali flunked.) The Corporal in charge passed out all the test papers, and I got my first taste of how trying this Army experience was going to be: For almost 15 minutes—so help me God this is true—the Corporal walked around the room intoning, "When filling out the line that says 'name', be sure and put your last name first and your first name last followed by your middle name or initial." He must have made that little speech at least twenty times—and at least ten guys had it wrong when he made his final check. Oh, brother, was this going to be a trial!

Next came the physical exam. There were about forty of us there, stripped down to our shorts, and we were told to line up in a straight line and to count off by twos—"One, Two, One, Two…" I came up number two, and the next thing I knew the same Corporal who had administered the written test was giving us our first assignment: "Okay," he said. "All you number ones will take your basic training at Fort Ord up near San Francisco where the weather is in the mid-sixties and you'll bivouac in the poppy fields near the golf course, and all you number twos will go to Camp Carson in Colorado." the corporal grinned evilly. "You're gonna love it at Carson—20 below with the wind chill most days during your eight-week stay, bivouacking in ten-feet of snow...A real winter wonderland, boys. You can make snowmen in your spare time. I envy you."

And then came the miracle I had been praying for. A little Asian doctor had been going down the line during the corporal's speech, listening to the recruits' heartbeats with his stethoscope, and the very second he put the stethoscope on my chest, my heart went off! A full-fledged attack of *paroxysmal tachycardia*! I crumpled to the ground, my heart racing, my body covered with sweat. The doctor turned to a nearby table where three medics were sitting and announced, somewhat worriedly, "This man has tachychardia!" One of the officers shuffled through the papers on the table, and held up a few sheets. "Yep," one said, "we've got letters here from his doctors. Send him home. He's 4-F." If my heart could have beaten any faster, it would have, such was the wave of joy that swept over me. That 48-hours of debauchery had saved my life! I rested on the floor for a couple of minutes, then got up and got dressed and rushed to get out of there before somebody changed his mind. I made one quick stop—at the blood-pressure station, and was terrified to learn my pressure was 190 over 115! The two young medics who took my pressure looked at each with alarm. "Get out of here, boy," said one. "Uncle Sam doesn't want to be responsible for your body!"

I called my father, who had just barely gotten home, and told him to come get me. The trip was off. He was elated, as, of course, was my mother—but nobody felt better about it than me. I'd have to find another apartment and buy a new car, but that sure beat the alternative.

At some point after the Vietnam War, the compulsory military service requirement—the draft—was dropped and we reverted to an all-volunteer military force. At least that's the status as this is being written.

Who knows what lies ahead, war-wise?

Show-biz, Here I Come!

Lots of young, aspiring writers have asked me over the years, "How did you break into the business?" Having a father who was a Hollywood writer-director certainly didn't hurt, but my show-biz break-through was a combination of talent, luck, hard-work, and luck.

I graduated from USC in June of 1955, and by August I was working on a Hollywood sound stage as a second-assistant director. (The show was called *Crossroads* and if you remember it, you really should get a life.) The job is as menial as it sounds, consisting of making out the daily call sheet, herding actors to and from their dressing rooms, hiring the extras, and generally trying to help the first assistant-director as much as you can. But I was thrilled to have the gig, in spite of the fact we worked six days a week, 12 to 14 hours a day. The money, for 1955, was great—a gross check of $208 a week found its way into my bank account, and best of all I was a part of the sacred and beloved business I had come to love.

There is no-where to go from being a second-assistant except to becoming a first-assistant or a production manager, and writing was what I wanted to do. So in my spare time (hah!) I slaved at my typewriter, knocking out short-stories and spec scripts of all types and genres. I did pretty well with the short-stories—several sales to second-tier men's magazines such as Gentleman, Dude, Chic, and the like. The scripts, however, languished in my drawer and all my father's influence couldn't land me a writing job.

The luck struck in late 1956 at a party given by a friend of mine. There was a young agent at the bash—his name was Bill Belasco, and he was related in some way to a very prominent New York theatrical family—and he took a liking to me right off the bat. He was frank to admit to me he was gay, which in those days really took a lot of courage, but it

51

Compliments of . . .

GRECO CABINET CORPORATION

2862 FULTON STREET
Brooklyn 7, N. Y.
TA 7-8111

LOCKE and RAPP
GAGS, BON MOTS,
DEATHLESS PROSE

WE DELIVER!

Los Angeles 46, California

Compliments of . . .

SUTPHIN STATIONERS, Inc.
PRINTING
OFFICE EQUIPMENT
I. Josephson
149-01 JAMAICA AVENUE
Jamaica 35, N. Y.

wasn't my body he was after, it was my mind. He knew of my father, of course, and after a half-hour conversation about my dreams of following in Dad's footsteps, he beckoned me to follow him into the bedroom. I balked—I thought I'd made it clear that I wasn't of that persuasion. No, no, he assured me. He was going to make a call and get me a job writing a script.

Into the bedroom we went, and a moment later Bill was on the phone with a close friend of his, a man named Jon Epstein, who was in charge of hiring writers at a studio called "Ziv Productions". Ziv was a syndicating outfit that churned out half-hour shows such as *Sea Hunt, Science Fiction Theater, Flipper* and the like. Bill gushed to his friend that he'd met a hot new talent—me—and asked Jon if he would give me a job. Bill guaranteed Jon he wouldn't be sorry. A few moments passed, and Bill, grinning ear to ear, passed me the phone. I introduced myself to Jon, and before I knew it he was telling me to come to his office Monday morning — he was going to assign me to write an episode of *Highway Patrol!* The pay was scale—$700—but I couldn't have been more thrilled if it had been a million! My writing career had begun, and I was determined not to blow the opportunity.

Thank God they loved the script I wrote for *Highway Patrol* (with only the slightest help from Papa) and put me under contract forthwith. In the next two years I wrote at least a hundred shows for that outfit, and the good news was that even though the pay remained at 700 a pop, 6 reruns were virtually guaranteed and in those days that meant an additional 150% of minimum. As much as I enjoyed my days at Ziv, however, I yearned for bigger and better things—comedy shows, that's what I wanted—but Bill deemed I wasn't ready yet.

He did, however, have a step-up in mind—that step being to leave Ziv and put myself onto the free-lance market where scale had now risen to 1100 bucks!

I found myself working steadily on shows like *Lassie, Peter Gunn, Brothers Brannigan, M-Squad* (where I wrote several episodes with a young up-and-coming talent named Robert Altman), and *Whirlybirds* — half-hour shows that were well thought of in their day. But I still craved a crack at comedy, which I was sure would come along sooner or later.

Around that time—1958—Bill Belasco died an untimely death (is there such a thing as a "timely death"?) in an automobile accident, and an agent at William Morris, Shelly Wile, romanced me with the promise of comedy-writing jobs. I signed with William Morris, and before the ink was dry Shelly came through.

"I've got a gig for you," he said. "A writer named Danny Simon has an assignment to write six episodes of a show called *Pete & Gladys*. He's getting three grand a script and he wants a young partner to bounce stuff off of—to mentor, if you will. He's willing to pay a grand a script, and I think you should jump at it."

And jump at it I did. Danny Simon was Neil Simon's brother, and a really top-notch comedy guy. He had been part of the staff of the Sid Caesar show in New York, working alongside Mel Brooks, Howie Morris, Sheldon Keller, and of course his brother Neil. I was a bit nervous about going to work with him—okay, I was a lot nervous. I mean, I was just a 24-year-old wet-behind-the-ears kid and he was a famous writer. But I proved up to the task, and by the third script we did together I was pulling my weight. And then I got another call from Shelly.

"They're starting a new show at Four-Star called *Peter Loves Mary*," he said, "and they're putting together a writing staff of four people—two teams. They've got one team from New York signed already—Mel Tolkin and Mel Diamond, and a third New Yorker, a playwright named Sam Locke who needs to find a partner." Shelly went on to tell me that the show was firm for 39 episodes, was to star Peter Lind Hayes and his wife, Mary Healy, and was being produced by a man named Billy Friedberg, whose last assignment had been as Producer of Phil Silvers' TV. classic, *You'll Never Get Rich*, better known as *Sgt. Bilko*. The three writers already aboard were going to make a thousand dollars a week, and Shelly had offered me up for 500. "But don't worry," he said. "It's a one-year guarantee, and if you can cut the mustard they'll bump you up to a G after the

first 13 weeks." I told Danny about the chance, and he was very support-
ive. "I hate to see you go," he said, "but if it doesn't work out, I'd love to
have you back with me."

So off I went with Shelly to meet with Billy Friedberg. We sat in
Billy's office for about 15 minutes, bantering and chatting about the show
and the world in general, and finally Billy looked at Shelly and nodded.
"If he's okay with Sam, he's okay with me," he said. My heart was racing.
"Where might I find Sam?" I asked, and Billy directed me to an office just
down the hall. "I'll be right back," I said, and scurried down the hall to
Sam's office. I opened the door and there, behind his typewriter, sat a little
curly-haired guy about 20-years my senior pounding away on a script.
"Are you Sam Locke?" I asked. "Yep," he said. "Well, I'm Joel Rapp, your
new partner," I said, and darted back to Billy's office where I grinned
broadly. "It's okay with Sam," I said, and we shook hands on the deal.

And thus began an 11-year partnership that was more like a marriage. A strong, happy marriage. I got my raise to a thousand week after
only six weeks on the job, and Sam Locke & Joel Rapp became one of the
most respected writing teams in the business. Together we wrote at least a
couple of hundred TV shows and a handful of B-movies under the pseud-
onym David Malcolm, a combination of our middle names. Sam had an
extraordinary wit and a fabulous sense of script construction, and best of
all he could recall in an instant the plot of any past movie or play ever
produced, a vitally important asset in the world of TV sitcoms. I think I
learned more about writing from Sam than anyone with the possible exception of my father, and although we broke up as a team in 1968 when
I decided to go off on my own and try for bigger things, he remained my
dearest friend until the day he died.

Me and the Mob

Way back in 1958 when I was a 24-year-old writer trying to make a name in the biz and just before I met and joined forced with Sam Locke, I got a call from Fred, a would-be producer friend of mine. "How would you like to write a script on the life on Roger "The Terrible" Touhy?" he asked. Now I knew who Touhy was—one of the most notorious gangsters of the Al Capone era in Chicago, and I also remembered I had recently read of his death at a ripe old age.

Fred told me that he had gotten a call from a group of guys in Chicago who wanted to make a movie glorifying Touhy's life and he'd been hired to produce it. If I agreed to write the script, it would mean $15,000 and a trip to Chicago to meet the "boys," who my friend made quite clear were members of the non-existent Mafia. I agreed at once—it sounded like a great adventure.

Within a week, Fred and I were on our way to Chicago. When we arrived, a limousine picked us up and delivered us to our hotel, a fancy place somewhere in the heart of downtown. There we met with three of the "boys," who instructed us that they wanted a script that depicted Touhy as he really was—a wonderful, soft-hearted guy who got a raw deal from the government and who was wrongfully incarcerated for many years up until he was released a few weeks before and then brutally murdered by unknown grudge-carrying mobsters. He was misunderstood, they said— in spite of the fact he himself had murdered several people, he was one of the truly nice guys, and that's how they wanted him to be portrayed.

So the next day arrangements were made for me to go to Stateville prison in Joliet and meet the warden. I forget his name, but he was a decent chap who took me on a tour of the prison, including a trip to the death chamber, following which we went back to his quarters for lunch.

Lunch, as I recall, was lovely, cooked by a convict and served by another con who was doing life for stabbing his wife to death. The main course was roast beef, which the killer-con deftly carved with a long, mean-looking knife, a fact I noted with some trepidation.

Armed with the warden's point of view about Touhy, which was basically a tale of an old, sick man whose "best" days were long behind him when he entered Stateville, I planned to spend another couple of days in Chicago doing research and then return home and write the script, armed with a check for $7500, the first half of the agreed-upon payment. The second $7500 would be paid to me upon receipt of the final script.

That night, Fred and I went to a party at the Chez Paree, a nightclub famous for its Mafia habitues and the home-away-from-home of a young publisher named Hugh Hefner, whose lavish apartment was only a few yards down the block. During the course of the evening I was approached by a very cheerful, disarming chap who introduced himself as Johnny Marshall. We talked for awhile about show-business—he was a big fan of "The Bickersons," my father's creation, and, like me, an avid golfer, and after having a couple too many drinks, I took him into my confidence: "Did you know,' I whispered, "that lots of these guys are in the Mafia?" He looked surprised, and shook his head. "How about that!" he said, then changed the subject. "How'd you like to play golf tomorrow at my club?" I was thrilled at the chance, and he said he'd have his car pick me up at ten o'clock in the morning. We shook hands and he went back to mingle among the guests.

Moments later, a white-faced Fred rushed over to my side. "Do you know who you were just talking to?" he asked. "Sure. A real nice guy named Johnny Marshall. We're going to play golf tomorrow. Why?" "His real name is Marshall Caifano," Fred said, "and here in Chicago he's Number One!"

My heart skipped a beat. He had seemed like such a nice, sweet guy.

Thank God the next morning dawned pouring rain. At about nine o'clock my phone rang. It was Johnny, apologizing for the rain and the obviously cancelled golf game, and then suggesting that when he came to the Coast next he would call me and we'd go play at my club, Hillcrest. I said great, gave him my number, and hung up.

About two months later I finished the script and sent it off to the "boys", who loved it and said there'd be a check for the balance in the mail shortly. Shortly turned into a week, two weeks, a month—and still no check. I finally decided the time had come to call up and find out what was causing the delay, and I was told by the head "boy" that they had decided the script stunk and they weren't going to pay me the rest and if I didn't like it, too bad.

What to do? These were bad guys, and since the whole project was sort of under the table, I didn't think it would be smart to bring in a lawyer.

Enter Johnny Marshall, who called to say he was in town and how about let's play golf tomorrow at Hillcrest? We set the time, and he showed up smiling ear to ear with his body-guard by his side. We teed off about 9:00—the bodyguard, named Elmer, declining to take off his black silk suit jacket in what was probably near hundred-degree weather—and about the sixth hole Johnny calmly asked me how it was going with the script. I told him about the problem, and he shrugged. "Oh, well," seemed to be his attitude. No more was said as we finished the round, repaired to the club-house for lunch and a couple of drinks, and then shook hands genially as off he went, Elmer at his side.

About an hour after I got home, the phone rang. It was Johnny. He thanked me profusely for a wonderful day, then casually asked me if I'd gotten the money yet. "What money?" "The seventy-five hundred those guys owe you." "Well, no..." I replied, somewhat bemused. "Well," said Johnny, "if you don't get a call from Western Union in the next hour, let me know." With that, we said our goodbyes and hung up.

Less than an hour later a call came from Western Union. Sure enough, a check for $7500 had just arrived from Chicago.

The next day, the paper carried a story that while Marshall Caifano, AKA Johnny Marshall, was playing golf at Hillcrest Country club, his arch-enemy was blown up by a car-bomb just outside of Chicago.

The story confirmed what I always had suspected—when it came to show business, it isn't what you know, it's who you know.

By the way, Johnny was arrested not long after for tax dodging and spent the rest of his life in prison.

The Roger Touhy story was never produced.

The Ghost of Lenny Bruce

This is really an eerie story.

It's about Lenny Bruce, a comedian best known for his having been arrested several times for using obscenity on stage, his daughter, Kitty, my one-time room-mate, and me.

Lenny, who died of a morphine overdose in 1966, was a friend of mine who was also a friend of my *best* friend at the time, an actor and announcer named Ronnie Gans. Being young and crazy and sharing a house in Hollywood, Ronnie and I made it a habit to go out almost every night to one of the night-clubs on the Sunset Strip where we watched comedians such as Mort Sahl, Shelly Berman, Buddy Hackett, Don Rickles and Lenny perform. Some nights we even managed to hit two or three spots, depending on our luck in trolling for dollies. (Of all these young comics, I thought Mort was the funniest—his humor was intellectual and often challenging, but in the long run he was the one who made me laugh the most. We actually shared an apartment for several months, but that's another story.) Ronnie and I became good pals of all the guys, and spent lots of time with them smoking dope, telling jokes, and conducting orgies…Remember, I said we were all young and crazy, and it was the 60s, after all!

At the time of his death Lenny was married to a woman named Honey and they had a daughter named Kitty who was about 6-years old in 1966 when Lenny died. I had met Honey a couple of times and had exchanged hellos with Kitty—but how much conversation can you have with a six-year-old kid?

Anyway, let's jump ahead to 1979, 13 years after Lenny's death. I was invited to a party somewhere in West Hollywood, and during the course of the evening a young woman came over to me and introduced herself. "My name is Kitty Bruce," she said. "Lenny's daughter. You're Joel Rapp, aren't you?" I acknowledged that I was, and we exchanged a little party banter, including my telling Kitty about my friendship with her father.

"Oh, I know all about it," she said. "Dad talks about you and Ronnie all the time. In fact, he asked me to say Hi if I ever ran into either of you guys someplace." I frowned. "What do you mean he talks about us all the time?" "Well," Kitty continued, "about once a month I go up to a special place on Mulholland Drive and Daddy comes and we sometimes talk about the old days for hours."

I began to suspect that Kitty had inherited, nay, improved upon Lenny's own mental ill-health and had definitely found his dope stash, but she went on bravely. "I'll never forget the story he told me about the time you guys…" And then, as God is my witness, she proceeded to relate three or four stories about times that Lenny and Ronnie and I spent together, including a very wild and crazy three-night bacchanal, the facts of which only the perpetrators would know. "Wait a minute," I said, cold chills crawling up my spine…"You don't believe me, do you?" she asked. "I know it's impossible for you to know those stories unless Lenny told you but it's even more impossible for a ghost to come down onto Mulholland and tell them to you!"

"You want to come up with me next time I go?" she asked in deadly earnest. "That way you can see him yourself."

I looked at this somewhat pretty, somewhat overweight young girl who was waiting intently for my answer, and I finally shook my head.

"No," I said. "I'd rather not." She shrugged and walked away, but not before she scribbled her phone number on a scrap of paper. "Okay," she said, "but call me if you ever change your mind." And she walked away.

To this day I'm baffled, and I can honestly say I didn't want to go up to Mulholland with her because I might have found out she was telling the truth!

Goodbye Bachelor Days— The First Time

Sometime in late 1958 I got a call from my good friend Roger Corman, who was well on his way to becoming the most famous of all B-picture producers, having made a couple of dozen low-budget exploitation features that had, each in its way, been a trail-blazing hit. I had already written and directed a couple of pictures for Roger—*High School Big Shot* and *T-Bird Gang* were their highly forgettable titles—but I had gotten my feet wet and was anxious to move ahead to something "better." Roger told me that he'd just completed a deal with some bankers in Puerto Rico to go down and shoot a movie there, and if I could come up with a good script that could be made on the really, really cheap we could go down there and shoot two pictures back to back, using the same crew on each. The idea of flying off for a few weeks to Puerto Rico appealed to me, and I told Roger I'd start looking for a property at once.

The very next day I found my property. It was a novella in *Esquire* magazine called "Expect the Vandals," a World War II story by an up-and-coming young writer, Philip Roth. Philip had recently published a book of short-stories under the title *Goodbye, Columbus*, and was presently working on his first novel—a book which I think was to become *Portnoy's Complaint*. Anyway, the *Esquire* piece was perfect for my needs—two American GIs are the only survivors of an abortive attack on a Pacific Island and find themselves marooned and hiding out from a large force of Japanese soldiers. One of the two men—a young man with a promising career as a pitcher in the Yankee organization— is crippled in the raid, and the other, an older, Jewish accountant is forced to take care of him while hiding from the Japs. Basically two characters and most of the action was in their hiding place, a cave—I did the math and figured I could make the picture for 35,000 dollars.

My movie writer/director debut

First things first. I contacted Roth's agent and bought the screen rights for a thousand bucks. I wrote the script, using almost all of Roth's brilliant dialogue, and then I set about raising the necessary cash. It wasn't hard—most of my father's friends chipped in and my room-mate, an aspiring young actor named Ronnie Gans, put in five-thousand dollars in exchange for the chance to play the part of the young pitcher. Roger had commissioned a script from a writer friend named Robert Towne called *It Came From Beneath the Sea* and we were good to go. (Towne went on to write several slightly more important works, foremost among them being his screenplay for *Chinatown*.)

I set off for Puerto Rico a few weeks later, with a stop in New York where I met with Philip Roth for a week at his Montauk home. I will never forget the long hours we spent sitting on the rocks near his house, overlooking a raging ocean and talking of our dreams. He was going to be a famous author and I was going to be a famous movie-maker. (Hey, one out of two ain't bad!). I left to join Roger and our gang in Puerto Rico convinced I was going to make an Academy Award winning film.

Things in Puerto Rico were not too terrific. Roger had put us up in a house he rented as opposed to the more expensive alternative of a hotel, so lots of the nearly thirty people on the shoot were sleeping on the floors and fighting to use one of the house's two or three bathrooms. (Halfway through the filming Roger relented and moved us all into a hotel—I thought he would die at the thought of the additional expense, but he lived to tell the tale and make a couple of hundred more profitable pictures.) It was hotter than Hell in Puerto Rico and extremely humid to boot, and the air was filled with mosquitoes and chiggers who found my tender legs and arms irresistible bait. The shooting in the cave and environs was going well, but putting together a Japanese army was a problem.

Elaine and Danielle

We couldn't find an oriental (nowadays "Asian") to save our lives, so we outfitted the most Asian looking Puerto Ricans we could find in Japanese uniforms and made do. We were putting in 14 hour days and both cast and crew were near exhaustion. Rebellion seemed inevitable, although it never quite came to pass.

The one bright spot in all of this was Elaine Epstein. Elaine was a very pretty secretary from New York, and she was vacationing in Puerto Rico with a girlfriend. They were down for a couple of weeks and staying at the hotel where we were and I was taken with her the first day we met. At that time I was sharing a cute little house in West Hollywood with Ronnie, running the streets like the crazy bachelor that I was, waking up most mornings with a heavy-duty hangover and a stranger in my bed, and frankly I had started thinking about changing my life-style. I had been pondering what it would be like to get married and have some kids, so I was ripe for the picking when Elaine and I crossed paths.

We began a hot and heavy affair, and before she left to go home I found myself in love. I couldn't wait to finish shooting and get back to New York to pick up where we left off. It was almost six weeks later before we finally wrapped everything up, and the next day I was in the Bronx

meeting Mr. and Mrs. Epstein, a lovely, *hamish* couple who were polar opposites from the show-business types I usually encountered. Well, not exactly. Larry Epstein was a projectionist in one of the local theaters, so I guess he qualified as a member of the biz.

The romance thrived, and we were married in a lovely ceremony in 1959. Elaine moved to California, followed closely by her parents, but it turned out that my romantic notions had frankly been misplaced. Neither one of us was really ready for marriage, but we stuck it out for seven years and although we went through a bitter divorce and custody battle in 1966, time *does* heal all wounds and we are friends today.

Of course, you pretty much have to be friends with a woman who bore you two beautiful daughters, one of whom has given us two beautiful grand-daughters. Daughters Lisa and Danielle and grandkids Hannah and Sophie made all the marital tribulations more than worthwhile, believe me.

Oh, by the way—the movie was re-titled *The Battle of Blood Island*, and although it didn't win an Academy Award, it got pretty good reviews, it was bought by a major studio and went out as the bottom half of a double bill with a really good movie, *Compulsion*. It played in the theaters on and off for a couple of years and then had a respectable run on television for several more years. My investors recouped their $35,000, but not much more as Roger has always been a sensational book-keeper. But what the heck—if I hadn't gone to Puerto Rico and made the movie, there's be no Lisa or Danielle or Hannah or Sophie. Talk about a huge return on an investment!

Our Hitch With *McHale's Navy*

During the 12 years of our writing partnership, Sam Locke and I had some really colorful experiences with producers and story editors. I'll never forget the day we sat with ten other writers and watched the pilot screening of *Gilligan's Island* wherein at the end the question on everybody's lips was, "That was great, Sherwood (Schwartz)—now what are you going to do next week?" Obviously, he thought of something! Or the scripts we wrote for Roger Corman in two or three days which have gone on to become "cult favorites." Or having to finish a one-hour comedy starring Bob Hope over the weekend of President Kennedy's assassination while everyone else in the world was glued to the TV. But one writing experience, having to do with *McHale's Navy*, deserves telling in these pages.

Sometime in late 1963, during a time in which we were under contract to Universal Studios, the TV brass decided they wanted to put together a "service comedy," a la the highly successful Phil Silvers' vehicle, *Sgt. Bilko*. Jennings Lang, a long-time producer at the studio (maybe best remembered for a scandal wherein he shot Producer Walter Wanger in an agency parking lot for allegedly fooling around with his wife, actress Joan Bennett) and former "Bilko" helmer Ed Montaigne were in charge of the project, and Sam and I were selected to help develop the show. After several weeks, (and a couple of other writers) we had developed a premise and a set of characters: The show would be set in the Pacific during the Japanese War on a mythical island called "Taratupa." The main characters would be a PT-boat commander named Quinton McHale, his diverse crew of loony sailors, a wacky ensign named Chuck Parker, and McHale's bete-noirs, Captain Wally Binghamton and his sidekick, Lieutenant Carpenter. The basic idea was that each week McHale and his gang would engage in some kind of sub-rosa hanky-panky which Captain Binghamton would try to thwart

The cast of *McHale's Navy*.

with no success. (Sound familiar, Bilko fans?)

So a pilot was written, the show was sold and slotted, and Sam and I were contracted to write 13 episodes out of each 39. (We had been offered the job of story-editors, but opted for the writing assignments instead, which left us free to work on other shows such as *Donna Reed*, *Gilligan's Island*, etc.) A writer named Si Rose was tapped for the associate-producer/story editor job, and after a brief meeting with Si, Sam and I went off to write our first script of the series.

We handed in the script and waited breathlessly for Si's reaction. (Even established writers such as Sam and I were always insecure about our work and were nervous wrecks until we heard good news from our various producers.) About a week passed and then the call came from Si. The conversation went something like this:

"Are you sure you guys are members of the Writer's Guild?" he asked. "Of course," we replied. "Why would you ask?" "Because," Si replied, "I have never seen such an amateur script from two professionals. In the first place," he continued, "the characters are all completely wrong." "But Si," we protested, "we *invented* those characters! How could they be wrong?"

"Look," he said, "I don't want to discuss the problems over the phone. Come in for a meeting tomorrow afternoon—and by the way, bring in some ideas for your next script."

Sam and I were completely bewildered. First of all, we thought the script was really funny—but if Si hated it so much, why was he talking about us doing another one? Sure, we had a contract, but contracts had been known to be settled.

Well, we went to the meeting, and after almost three hours during which Si went through the script line by line, criticizing almost everything, we went home and went to work on an enormous re-write. Hoping for the best, we handed in the revised script, and when the final shooting script was delivered to us about a week later, we were shocked: The mimeographed copy contained about 85% of our original, "amateurly written" first draft, about 10% of the re-written material, and another 5% of stuff Si had seen fit to add. We were stunned. Why had he put us through that grinding re-write if he were going to use almost the entire first draft??

Well, to make this story as short as possible, we continued to turn out scripts and Si continued to demean them, ask for complete re-writes, and then finally revert back almost completely to the original drafts. It drove me crazy, and after about the first ten scripts I wanted to walk away, but cooler-head Sam talked me out of it and we labored on. We felt better when we found out the three other teams writing the show were getting the same treatment from Si, but still…For three solid years we'd been hearing Si's rantings—"This script stinks!" "I've never read anything this terrible!" "Don't you guys know this is supposed to be a comedy??" And worse…

Finally, in 1966 Sam and I handed in our thirty-ninth script, which was to be the final episode of the hugely successful three-year run. We waited for the inevitable phone call from Si, and when it came we went to the meeting expecting the usual excoriation. Here, as God is my witness, are Si's exact words as he lifted the script from his desk and looked us in the eyes:

"Boys," he said, "I'm terribly disappointed. This script just isn't up to your usual standards."

Huh????

Did I hear you say you wanted to be in show-business?

Ernest Borgnine Exposed

Speaking of *McHale's Navy*…

Sam and I had been working on *McHale's Navy* for a year at least, and in that time we had never visited the set or met any of the cast members. Until New Year's Eve, 1965…

Sam was giving a New Year's party at his home on Nichols Canyon in the Hollywood Hills, when at about 11:30 the doorbell rang and I went to open it. There, in the flesh, stood Commander Quinton McHale himself—Ernie Borgnine. He greeted me with a big smile and stuck out his hand. "Hi," he said. "I'm Ernie Borgnine. I saw there was a party going on here and if you don't mind I'd like to come in."

I quickly explained to Ernie that the host and I were members of the show's writing staff, co-creators as a matter of fact. "Of course," he beamed, recognizing our names. "What a fabulous coincidence." And with that, he marched into the living room, introduced himself to several of the guests, then made himself comfortable on the couch, sipping from the drink in his hand and wolfing down the hors d'oerves on the table, and told the interested gathering the following tale:

"When I was a young boy," he said, "my mother, may she rest in peace, told me that there was an old family tradition in the Borgnine family. On New Year's Eve, she said, if you see a party in progress, even if it's at the home of strangers, knock on the door and ask if you might ring in the New Year with them. This will bring you, and all the guests at the party, great good luck and a wonderful New Year!"

Well, we all thought it was a charming and wonderful story, and spent the next hour or so chatting with Ernie about this, that, and the other thing until finally, about one-o'clock, he got up, thanked Sam for having him into the party (and thanking both of us for all the "wonderful scripts") and left.

Are you ready for the punch line?

The next morning, in one of the Hollywood gossip columns, the following item appeared (I'm paraphrasing): "It wasn't a very Happy New Year for Ernie Borgnine and wife Katy Jurado. Seems the Borgnine's were in attendance at a party in the Hollywood Hills when suddenly, sometime before the witching hour, the two had a huge, screaming fight that was probably heard all the way down to Hollywood Boulevard. The enraged Ernie stormed out of the party and disappeared for almost two hours before he finally came back and escorted the still steaming Mrs. B. home."

Family tradition, indeed! As my old pal Sidney Skolsky used to say, "But don't get me wrong. I love Hollywood!"

Bob Hope the Actor—Not!!

Although Bob Hope, who at this writing just celebrated his 100th birthday, will always be in the pantheon of great comedians (and why not? My Uncle Johnny worked on his writing staff for 17 years!) there's little wonder he never won that coveted Academy Award for acting.

I discovered just how wanting was Hope's thespianic ability during the shooting of a *Chrysler Theater* TV Show back in 1962. Sam Locke and I had written a comedy script (the title escapes me) which we had hoped to sell as a feature film, but when Mort Lachman, Bob's head writer and producer of his TV filmed specials read it and wanted to buy it for Hope, we sold.

We were excited, to say the least. Although Hope was the host for the series of one-hour dramatic anthology shows, he himself was contracted to star in two of the 32 each season, and having our story chosen as one was an honor, not to mention a very hefty pay-day. The story concerned a Hugh Hefner-type guy (Hope), editor of a *Playboy*-type magazine, who was being attacked by a moralistic-type woman who was running for Congress on a platform which included getting rid of Bob and his trashy publication. (You remember those old Doris Day-Rock Hudson movies where the puritanical girl hated the racy bachelor—until they met, of course, and fell in love? Well, that was pretty much the thrust of our story.)

Anyway, the part of the woman was specifically described as a 35ish, intellectual type, and we should have known we were in some sort of trouble when Bob asked that Jill St. John (his flame at the time) be given the role. Jill St. John, 22-years old and the ultimate screen sex-pot, playing that goody-two-shoes Congressional candidate? God help us—even if they put glasses on her it made no sense. Luckily, cooler heads prevailed, and an Academy

Uncle Johnny with Bob Hope, 1965

Award winning actress, Eva Marie Saint, was cast in the part. A real coup, as Ms. Saint was, and still is, considered one of America's greatest performers.

Well, one day Sam and I decided to go down and visit the set and watch them shoot a few scenes It was something we rarely did, but we wanted to watch this fabulous actress in action.

Well, here's what we saw: Bob and Eva Marie playing a scene together—with Bob looking over her shoulder and reading every one of his lines off of cue cards!   And guess what? The dialog came out sounding like someone reading their lines off cue cards, surprise, surprise! We couldn't believe our eyes, or our ears. And frankly, neither could Ms. Saint. We could tell she was furious, but to her everlasting credit she kept her temper and turned in a wonderful performance.

The show got great reviews, but Sam and I never again saw a Bob Hope movie without being aware that somewhere, nearby, was a person holding up cardboard rectangles with all his dialog written out in bold, black strokes.

Thanks for the memory, Robert!

Match Please, Darling

One of the most rewarding, not to mention educational, experiences of my life was writing a play with my father. It was called *Match Please, Darling*, and it ran for almost five months at the Coronet Theater on La Cienega Boulevard here in Los Angeles.

It was 1967, and it came about this way:

I had driven up to my father's palatial Beverly Hills manse fully prepared for the conversation I knew to be inevitable; to wit, borrowing money. I winced as my father's words spilled out. "Son," he said, "do you suppose you might lend me a few dollars till next Wednesday?" "What about the twenty you still owe me, Dad?" I asked. "I can't pay you this week," he said sheepishly. "That's what you told me *last* week!" was my response. "Well," he bellowed, "I kept my word, didn't I?"

But seriously…I have already discussed my father's legendary profligacy, but he'd reached a stage in his life where he wasn't interested in working anymore and he and Mom were living off her shrewd stock and real-estate investments. I could tell he was bored with his life of golfing and losing at gin every day after lunching with his pals at the legendary Hillcrest round table, so I thought it would be a good thing for him psychologically to get his hand back in and write something. With that in mind, I put forth a proposition. "Pop," I said, "I've got this idea for a play which is about a man and wife and an interfering couple upstairs and a Playboy Bunny and a lawyer who's a degenerate gambler, and I think you and I could have fun writing it together. We'd be the first father and son playwriting team since—well, since forever, and I really think it could be a very funny piece." He was frowning with some degree of interest, but he was far from convinced, so I applied what turned out to be the *coup d'grace*— "And best of all, we can make the husband and wife John and

73

The playwright and his director

Blanche Bickerson and incorporate lots of their famous routines!"

That sold him, and the next day we began blocking the play. I was alive with anticipation, excited by the prospect of working with a genuine master of comedy, my comedy-writing idol if truth be known. I soon learned, however, that collaborating with one's father would not be all peaches and cream. I arrived at this conclusion the first time I suggested one of my jokes was funnier than one of his.

His eyes narrowed. "What did you say?" "I said I think my joke in this spot is better than yours." "You really think so?" he asked quietly. I nodded. "All right, son." Then, suddenly, "Go to your room!" "But Dad—" "I said go to your room. " I sighed resignedly. "I lost my head, Pop. Your joke *is* better than mine, no doubt about it." "That's a good boy," he beamed, and our first crisis was over.

And so it went. His jokes were always better than mine, either under the threat of bed without dinner or two weeks without my allowance of other things equally terrifying to a 33-year-old man with a wife and two children. Of course there were other problems, like the conflict between my father's era and my own.

The most amusing example of this occurred during the construction of what turned out to be the laugh-filled show's biggest laugh, where John Bickerson is alone in his apartment in his pajamas with a sexily attired Playboy bunny. It's all perfectly innocent, but you can imagine John's embarrassment when Blanche comes in and sees her husband in bed with a voluptuous authentically costumed Playboy Bunny seated on the edge. The Bunny stands up, John jumps out of bed guiltily, and the audience roars. After the first preview of the show, my father said, "Son, I've got an inspiration! A great line for John." "What is it?" I asked. "He turns to the bunny," said my father, "and says, 'A package of Wings, please.'" I stared. "A package of what?" "Wings, you dum-dum! Cigarettes. Don't you get the joke?" "Oh," I said, starting to chuckle. "Hey, that is funny. But we better not make it Wings, Pop. We better make it a more modern brand...like, say...a package of Marlboros?"

Grudgingly, he acceded, and just as I figured, every night when John Bickerson asked the Playboy Bunny for a package of Marlboros, the house came down. The funniest part is that to his dying day, my father still thought it was his joke!

Working with Dad was truly amazing. I thought I'd mastered the art of comedy construction, especially with Sam Locke mentoring me on a daily basis—but I learned during the course of the next few weeks that I still had a long way to go. It was incredible learning experience to see what lines got laughs and which ones didn't. I was amazed at some of the surprises and Dad spent lots of time with me explaining why certain things worked and others didn't. Unlike TV, where we were guaranteed mirth by the use of canned laughter, the theater was a whole new ball game, and it taught me more about comedy than I'd learned in my whole prior career.

My father directed the play himself and it got excellent reviews. Actually our entire family got into the act: My brother Paul manned the ticket booth, my mother sold sodas and muffins during the two intermissions, and at some point during the run I stepped into the role of Harvey, the gambling lawyer, a part I had tailored for myself from the start. Audiences roared at the play on a nightly basis—there were literally more laughs in "Match" than in a nearby production of "The Odd Couple", a fact I can vouch for because I went to their show and clocked the laughs myself. During our five-month run we came very close several times to our goal of mounting a Broadway production, but it never came to pass and since we were only breaking even every week, we decided to close the show.

Although not an actor by profession, I had a knack for the craft and was really enjoying myself playing Harvey until one day during a brush-up rehearsal. I read a line in a way I thought was extremely funny, and suddenly the director bellowed, "No, no, you idiot, that's all wrong! It'll never get a laugh that way!" "But, sir…" I began to protest. "Listen, kid," said the director menacingly, "either you read the line my way or else!"

My shoulders sagged and I nodded. "Yes, Dad. Anything you say." I was damned if I was going to suffer through another night without my milk and cookies.

The Wedding of the Century

After Elaine and I were divorced, I spent almost four years back on the streets again, once more running wild—wine, women and song being the order of those days. My career was going well—Sam Locke and I were churning out sitcom scripts as fast as our fingers could fly over the typewriter—multiple segments of shows like *Donna Reed, The Flying Nun, The Patty Duke Show, Gilligan's Island, McHale's Navy*—but I wasn't really happy with the bachelor life. I was living alone in a rented house on Mulholland Drive, the divorce from Elaine had turned very, very nasty—all the usual problems about money and child visitation were a constant thorn in my side, and frankly, I was lonesome for a steady companion and a real home and hearth. Then one morning I met the woman who would play an enormous role in the rest of my life.

It was in Nate 'n Al's Delicatessen in Beverly Hills, a fairly well-known watering hole where a couple of dozen of TV's hottest sitcom writers would gather almost every morning in four or five adjoining booths and spend a couple of hours drinking coffee and seeing who could top whom in the joke department. Most of these guys were very funny—guys you never heard of but the best comedy writers in the world, take my word for it. Guys like Jay Burton, Artie Julian, Al Gordon, Phil Sharpe, and Larry Klein, just to name a handful, would swap tales of life with Johnny Carson or Jack Benny or Bob Hope or whomever they happened to be writing for at the time. I was privileged to be part of that unforgettable clutch, and I must say I got in my share of zingers over the years.

Of all the guys, Jay was probably the funniest. His show-business stories were legion, but here's one I'll never forget: In case you didn't know, one of Milton Berle's claims to fame was the size of his...well, his member. According to those in the know, it could put a good-sized salami to shame. Well, one day Milton was approached by another Hollywood character also famous for his enormous size who challenged Milton to a cock-off to see who was actually bigger. The two men set up a meeting, complete with seconds of which Jay was one, and right before the big unveiling, Jay turned to Milton and said, "Just take out enough to win." Every morning Jay could be counted on to come up with the most and funniest one-liners, no easy task when you had a bunch of really witty egomaniacs dueling for the honors.

Anyway, one Saturday morning, on my way to a golf game with Artie Julian, I came into Nate n' Al's for a quick breakfast. Saturday mornings were quiet there, so I sat down in a booth with a doctor friend of mine and ordered pastrami and eggs, pancake style. A few minutes later, this really pretty dark-haired girl came in with a very young girl by her side. As they walked to a nearby booth, I looked at my doctor friend and nodded toward the striking brunette and the girl who turned out to be her 8-year-old daughter. "See that girl?" I said. "I'm gonna marry her!" Well, the doctor laughed because that's what most of us single guys always said whenever we saw a really good-looking woman, but this time I was really smitten at first sight. I finished my breakfast and walked over to the booth where she was sitting. "Hi," I said. "My name is Joel Rapp and you and I are going to get married." As she looked at me in amazement, I scribbled my phone number on a napkin and told her to call leave her name and number. "I'm running late for a golf game," I said, "but you and I are going out tonight so let me know where to pick you up." With that, I signaled the waitress to bring me her check, and left without ever even finding out her name.

When I got home from the game—I shot around 82 that day as I recall—there was a message. It was from Lynn Paul—"The girl you met this morning at Nate n' Al's"—and in it she gave me her phone number, her address, and said that 7:30 would be a perfect time to pick her up.

To say it was a whirlwind romance would be putting it mildly. It turned out she had just broken off a two-year relationship with Don Knotts (the sheriff on the Andy Griffith show?) and was ripe for a new relationship. I moved in with Lynn about two weeks later, and about a year later we decided to tie the knot.

Since we'd both been married before we decided to keep the wedding as simple as we could. We picked New Year's Eve, 1969, and made arrangements to fly up to Las Vegas for the ceremony, accompanied by

Lynn's two sisters and their husbands. We called our good friend Shecky Greene, one of America's top comedians at the time and a regular on the Las Vegas lounge circuit, and asked him if he would be Best Man and arrange for a Rabbi to perform the ceremony.

Shecky called us back a couple of days later with good news and bad news: The good news was he'd be thrilled to be our best man as long as we could put off the ceremony until he finished his final show at 2 a.m.— and the bad news his rabbi wouldn't marry us because we didn't have a "get", an official Jewish divorce. "Can you get a get?" he asked (we already smelled a comedy routine) and we told him time-constraints made it impossible but what the hell, we'd get married in one of Vegas's many little wedding chapels, and two o'clock in the morning would be just fine.

So we flew up to Vegas on New Year's Eve day and made all the arrangements: Wedding license and a reservation for a 2:30 a.m. wedding at a little chapel just outside of town. By 2 o'clock in the morning, after a wild day of gaming, we found ourselves headed for the chapel with an entourage of people following behind in three rented limousines. Somehow, during the several hours between our arrival in town and our departure for the chapel we'd picked up a crowd of "friends" eager to share the nuptial ceremony with us, Shecky, still stoked from his last performance and not a little "shicker" as we say in Yiddish, leading the way.

When we arrived at the chapel, called The Wee Church of something or another, I forget now, we were greeted by a gorgeous, buxom red-headed woman who informed us that the Reverend Billy-Joe, the minister who would perform the ceremony, would be just a little bit late. He was still at the local radio station finishing up his nightly program. Jeez! A radio preacher was going to marry us! Aw, what the heck. It was Vegas, after all.

Our group of about 20 people headed into the chapel where Shecky began his third show of the evening, funnier by far than either of his two regular gigs. Outside, in the foyer, Lynn and I were signing the papers and when we finished the paperwork we asked about the price. "Well," said the red-head, who I decided was a show-girl or a hooker who had this night job to supplement her income, "we have three different selections: For $35 dollars you can get plastic flowers for the bride and groom plus a Polaroid photo, piped-in music and an audiotape of the ceremony; For $25 there'd be flowers, piped in music and a photo; and for $10 Billy Joe will lead the vows in a five-minute ceremony, period." I reached into my pocket and pulled out a ten-dollar chip. "We'll take the no-frills ceremony," I said, and the woman looked at me with disdain. "I'm sorry," she said, "This is a wedding chapel. We don't take chips." I looked at her in shock. "Come on," I said. "This is Vegas! Everybody takes chips! Chips is money!" She was adamant. No chips. So I borrowed ten dollars from Lynn and paid her, just as Billy Joe came in, all smiles.

After the introductions and a caution to Billy Joe that he could mention God but please leave the Kid out of it, we went into the chapel and the ceremony began. Well, the five-minute ceremony took almost half-an-hour thanks to Shecky's incessant commentary. I must say it was one of the funniest half-hours he ever did, and believe me when I tell you he was one funny guy.

When the ceremony was finally over and the wedding guests and Shecky had trooped outside to the waiting limousines, Lynn and I stopped at the door and shook hands with Billy Joe. "Thanks, Rev," I said, then put my hand into my pocket and pulled out the ten-dollar chip. "I'd really like to give you a little gratuity, but all I have is this chip." Before I could take another breath Billy Joe had grabbed it. "That's okay," he said, dripping with Southern charm, "I take chips!"

With that, Lynn and I stepped outside, only to find all the limousines had already left. There we were, basically just beginning our honeymoon, stranded in the middle of no-where without a taxi in sight.

To his everlasting credit, Billy Joe drove us back to our hotel, where we took up where we left off at the gambling tables, and to this day I'm sick that I didn't spring for an audio-tape. Oh, well.

Is it any wonder the marriage didn't work?

Golfing With Gable

Although this story doesn't have a particularly whopping punch line, this is, after all, a compilation of my most vivid memories and this particular memory is as vivid as it gets. It's about my nine holes with Clark Gable, whom I worshiped above all movie stars, male or female. That's right, even more than Esther Williams, Hedy Lamarr, Jane Powell, Lana Turner, Ava Gardener, and several other glamorous stars of the 30s, 40s, and 50s. I had seen every movie he ever made, most of them several times, and had even built a little "shrine" to His Majesty in my West Hollywood house—mostly pictures from his various films, the centerpiece being an original studio oil portrait depicting Clark as Rhett Butler from Gone with the Wind. I could quote entire scenes from many of his flicks, and I had developed a rather good imitation of Gable if I do say so myself.

The big day occurred in 1959 when I was 25-years old. I was a member of Hillcrest Country Club—actually, my father was a member and I had filial privileges—and during those years I was a fairly good golfer. I got down as low as a 7 handicap, which means my average game was in the high 70s or low 80s. (Today I can still play in the 70s & 80s, but now we're talking about the temperature, not my scores.) One after-noon I came out alone, and with my bag slung over my shoulder I went over to the first tee, prepared to play 9 holes. The starter told me I had a choice—I could play the front side by myself, or I could join Mr. Schwartz and his guest on the 10th hole where they were just about to tee off. I always preferred to play with other people if only to show off my prodi-gious drives and excellent short game, so I hustled over to the 10th tee where I saw Mr. Schwartz teeing up his ball, while standing next to him, in a polo shirt and shorts, was—you guessed it. Gable himself.

My knees were quivering like a schoolgirl as I rushed up to the tee. "May I join you?" I asked Mr. Schwartz, who was a good friend of my father's and with whom I had played a couple of rounds in the past. "Of course," he said. "It's a pleasure to have you." With that, I turned to Gable and extended my sweating hand. "Hi," I said, "my name is Joel Rapp." "Hi," he said, in his best Gable manner, "I'm Clark Gable." I looked at him wide-eyed. "Of course you are," I said, and he burst out laughing. I was really taken aback by the fact he had felt he had to introduce himself. I mean, he was Clark Gable for goodness sakes!

Well, the next couple of hours were some of the best times of my life. I played exceptionally well, despite my nervousness, and by the twelfth tee I had worked up the courage to do my Gable impression on the man himself. "Good shot, sweetheart," I said in my finest Gablese, and to my everlasting joy, CG laughed like crazy. "That's a pretty good impression," he said, and so for the rest of the round Mr. Schwartz played golf with two Clark Gables. At some point we laughed about how almost every comic in the world who did impressions did Gable. "Who do you think does you best?" I asked. "Well I do, of course!" he said, and it was true. By this time he really *did* sound like someone doing an impression of him. "But I'd have to say Rich Little comes in second."

I came away from the round floating on air. I don't remember exactly what I shot, but I do remember Clark Gable signed my scorecard. I have it somewhere to this day, although I'm not sure where, and despite the urging of some of my pals, even if I find it you'll never see it listed for sale on e-Bay. Like they say on those Mastercard commercials, some things are priceless.

The Birth of 'Mother Earth'

PART ONE

The actual seed for the birth of "Mother Earth" was planted in 1968 the day I quit my job as Director of Comedy Development at Universal Pictures. What an adventure *that* was—a Hollywood urban legend if ever there was one.

I got the job through a friend of mine, Stu Erwin, Jr. (His father, Stu Erwin, was a comic actor way back when, who had a TV show of his own in the 1950s). Stu and I had gone to high-school together, and I was thrilled and delighted when my agent called and told me that Stu, an executive at Universal, had selected me to become his new Director of Comedy Development, a job that would pay me 1500 dollars a week, in those days an absolute ton of money. I went to meet with Stu in his office in the Big Black Tower as the main Universal building was known, and he laid down the ground rules for my new job: "I have given you a spacious office in the back of the lot," he said. "Couches, chairs, a patio, a secretary, a refrigerator, the works. I want you to start collecting potential properties to be developed as comedy television pilots or feature films. Take all the time you need, and when you feel you have a goodly supply of viable ideas, bring them up to my office and we'll pick and choose the projects with which to proceed. I don't want to see your face or hear your voice until you're ready," he concluded. We shook hands, and off I went.

I repaired to my office, introduced myself to my secretary, and began my task with hugely genuine enthusiasm. I was determined to find several properties that could be developed into hits, thus insuring my financial future as well as making a few bucks for Stu and Universal. I called every comedy writer and agent that I knew and asked them to send me material, and within a few weeks I had scripts and treatments and proposals all over my desk, my couch, and the floor. I conscientiously read every single presentation, and after about six weeks I felt I had winnowed the material down to a manageable size.

I marched up to the Stu's office in the Black Tower, carrying my package of material cradled in my arms like a baby, and smiled broadly at his secretary. "Hi," I said. "I've come to deliver this package to Mr. Erwin." His secretary frowned. "Hmmm," she said. "That might be a problem since Mr. Erwin is no longer with us." I almost dropped the baby right onto its head. "Mr. Erwin is what???" I exclaimed. "He left last week to become vice-president of Grant Tinker Entertainment," she said. "Sorry." That'll teach me not to read the Trades, I thought, then I looked around in dismay. "So what am I supposed to do with my package?" I asked. She shrugged. "Don't ask me," she said. "I only work here."

Baffled, I carried my package down the hall to the office of another top exec, Frank Price, who later became the President of some studio or another. I explained the problem to Frank, and asked him what I should do. "Laddie," he whispered, "if I were you I'd take that stuff back to my office and lay low until somebody calls." "You mean just keep on taking the checks and doing nothing?" I asked, incredulous. "Shhh," said Frank. "You didn't hear that from me..."

So that's what I did. For weeks and weeks I hid out in my office, hearing from no-one except the paymaster with his 1500 bucks every week. I spent my days waving at the tour trams which passed right by my patio every half-hour or so, smoking lots of dope, and reading like crazy. (My friends suggested I write something on spec as long as I was at it, but go find a writer who'll work on spec when he's making a big fat paycheck.) At some point I stopped coming in altogether, checking with my secretary four or five times a day from the golf course just to see if anybody called. Nobody did. It was a scene right out of old Hollywood, a story I'd heard before but always deemed to be apocryphal. I felt sorry for my secretary, who had nothing to do all day but sit and read paperback romance novels, but she was happy and so life went on.

One day I called in and there was actually a message: "There's a meeting tomorrow of all executives," she said. "Ten o'clock in the Tower...and wear a suit and tie." I knew I had a suit and tie someplace, so I told her to RSVP on my behalf. I figured I'd finally be revealed as a fraud and it would be my last day at Universal, but little did I know just how it would play out.

I showed up promptly at ten and entered the conference room where about a dozen black-suited executives were seated. The President of the studio, Sid Scheinberg, was at the head of the table, and once the coffee and croissants were delivered, the meeting began. The agenda was next season's TV schedule, and at least a half-hour into the confab not a word had been addressed to me. Maybe I actually was going to escape with my job and my paycheck intact. The discussion went on for about an hour, how to change or improve this show and that, and I found myself staring out the window as I listened to what I considered to be totally mindless chatter about totally irrelevant stuff. (The fact that I'd smoked a big, fat joint right before the meeting hadn't exactly put me in a serious state of mind.) At some point they got to talking about *Ironside*, a show starring Raymond Burr as a detective confined to a wheelchair. They wanted to try and squeeze another season out of the show, and somebody suggested that if Ironside got married it might open up a whole new area for additional episodes. "What do you think, Joel?" Sid's voice snapped me out of my reverie. "Well," I responded, "if you're talking about him marrying that beautiful blonde assistant of his, that's boring. But if you want to hook him up with that black guy that pushes his chair...." There was a sudden deafening silence in the room. Everybody knew that Raymond Burr was gay, but I guess I was pushing the envelope. "That's not funny, Joel," Sid said sternly. "We're not here to play games."

And then I did the stupidest thing I ever did in my whole life—which turned out to be the smartest but I didn't know it then. I stood up, and made a pronouncement: "I can't take this anymore," I said. "All this talk about a bunch of stupid TV shows that are going to be the same shit as all the other stupid TV shows while the whole world is falling apart right outside that window. Where do I go to quit?" Sid glared at me for a moment, and then nodded toward the door. "Down the hall to Bernie Shwartz's office," he said. "Third door on the left." And with that, I left the room.

I finished my business with Bernie, then stopped by my agent's office to tell him I'd quit my job. I thought he would have a heart attack. After all, the $150 a week he was collecting in my commission was paying his secretary *and* his phone bill. He went into a tirade and begged me to reconsider, but I was adamant. "That's it for me," I said. "I'm quitting the TV business forever. I'm going to go home, write a movie script that's been percolating for months, and see what happens."

When I got home and told Lynn of the morning's events, she was stoic. "That was very noble," she said. "Standing up for your principles and all. But just as a footnote—what are we going to do for money?" I looked at her, incredulous. "Are you kidding?" I asked. "Aren't we rich? We've got this beautiful home, and two brand-new cars, and a maid..." "And a mortgage, and car payments, and alimony payments, and child support payments..." I frowned, just a bit taken aback. "Not to worry," I finally said. "I've got this great idea for a screenplay and when I sell it we'll be the chips for life."

So I set to work on the screenplay, an autobiographical piece about my divorce and remarriage and all the horrific events that transpired therein, and when I finished I gave it to my agent who called in the middle of the night to pronounce it a masterpiece. "What do you want me to do with it? he asked. "Get it to George Cukor," I said. "I want him to direct." (George Cukor was a multiple Academy Award winning director who was best known for his success directing women.) Since my picture basically was about the battle between a man and two women, he had been my choice to direct from the git. The fact he was almost 80-years old was not a factor. He was still reported to be vibrant and anxious to work.

We sent the script to Mr. Cukor, who called and asked that we meet him at his house for breakfast the following morning. In what was truly one of the most memorable days of my life, we arrived at Mr. Cukor's lavish Beverly Hills home to be greeted by a butler and led through a series of beautifully decorated rooms studded with photographs from his legendary career. Greer Garson, Vivian Leigh, Barbara Stanwyck, Jane Wyman, Joan Crawford...the walls were covered with photos of the diminutive director with almost every star in the Hollywood firmament.

The butler led us out to the patio, which overlooked the pool and a lovely, manicured garden, and the Master himself arose from his seat at a linen-covered table to greet us warmly. We sat down amidst the splendor of the setting, not to mention the sterling silver and the crystal, and after a moment or two of introductory banter, Mr. Cukor looked at me and pronounced, "Son, you have written a flawed masterpiece." I almost fainted with delight before I recovered my senses and asked him what the flaw was. He explained, but assured me it was nothing that couldn't be remedied in a re-write, and as the white-gloved butler served us our exquisite breakfast, Mr. Cukor asserted that he'd love to direct the picture. "One problem, however," he said. "I've made a commitment to Elizabeth Taylor to direct a picture called "The Blue Bird" in Austria, and if it goes, which at this point is still up in the air, I'll be hors d'combat for at least a year, and frankly I'm not getting any younger." He told us he'd know about the Taylor picture in the next couple of weeks—two weeks which I spent never uncrossing my fingers unless I was praying.

Alas, the Taylor deal went through, and George Cukor was out of the picture, literally and figuratively. I was crushed, and after my agent sent it out to a couple of other directors who turned it down I told him to file it and forget it. I needed some time to think about my next move in life.

PART TWO

And now we finally get to the Mother Earth part of this story.

It was October, 1970. By that time we had spent most of our savings, meager as they turned out to be, and we were literally down to our last two grand in the bank. Much of that money had been spent on houseplants, since Lynn and I had fallen in love with the houseplant experience several years before, long before anybody but little old ladies with tennis shoes were into indoor gardening. We had invested a fortune buying plants that died because they weren't really meant to live inside. (In those days, when you visited a nursery, if you could lift a plant up the help would assure you it would thrive indoors.) But through constant trial and error, we had finally discovered which plants would live and which wouldn't, and as a result our house was a veritable jungle of tropical greenery. People used to joke that they'd best bring a machete when they came to visit the Rapps. Anyway, we had invited our friends Nora and Larry Marks to dinner one fateful night—Larry was one of the best comedy writers in Hollywood, a regular contributor to M*A*S*H among many other shows—and I was discussing our financial plight.

"Things are so bad," I said, turning to a Boston fern by the side of the couch where I was sitting, "that I'm either going to have to eat this fern or sell it, and if you've ever tasted a fern frond..."

"Tell you what," said Larry. "That fern's sort of pretty. I'll give you ten bucks for it." Lynn jumped to her feet. "What??" she practically shouted. "Ten bucks for a fern I raised from a spore? Ten bucks for a fern I sang to at night when it was a baby, a fern I cleaned up after it spilled its water ration on the floor...I wouldn't take a penny less than twenty!"

MOTHER EARTH AND FATHER JOEL—While husband Joel talks to "offspring," Lynn (also known as Mother Earth) plays at watering plants outside the Mother Earth Plant Boutique.
Times photo by Kathleen Ballard

TV Writer Thriving in Grow Biz

Mother Earth's first big break. (Courtesy of *Los Angeles Times*)

"Fifteen," said Larry. "Sold", said Lynn, and Lynn and Joel Rapp were in the plant business!

The four of us spent the rest of the night, literally until almost seven o'clock in the morning, mapping out our plan: We would rent a little store someplace and we'd set it up to look like our living room We would stock only the plants that we knew would live, and we would plant them in fun, unusual, funky containers like we had many of our own—a philodendron spilling out of a trumpet, a dwarf palm thriving in an antique tobacco tin, a discarded sink overflowing with maidenhair fern....And to top it all off, we would tag each plant with a little card which would bear something to the effect of this message: "Hi. My name is Freddie. I'm your new pothos plant. Keep me in indirect light, water me when my soil is dry, love me, and I will thrive." The name shtick was critical. We guessed that if you got a plant with a card that says, "Hi, my name is Fowler," you don't have a plant anymore, you have a child. It meant the owner would get up every morning and say, "Hi, Fowler, how're you doin'?" And maybe notice a little spot of brown or feel that the soil is too dry....you would pick up little signs of trouble, nip them in the bud, and the plants that used to die on you would live. We would turn on the world to the houseplant experience. If we could do it, anybody could. The press would flock to the store and we'd become famous...I saw the headlines before my eyes..."TV Writer Thriving in Grow-Biz"...

My role model was Hugh Hefner, who started Playboy with five hundred bucks. I envisioned that someday there would be a huge building somewhere with the name "Mother Earth" lighting up the sky. There would be Mother Earth products on every nursery shelf in America, and Lynn and I would be rolling in dough. Larry and Nora were eager to finance the deal, but we didn't want them to risk their money on such a crazy, wild, longshot of an idea (although both Lynn and I were convinced it was a sure thing) so Lynn sold her mink coat to Nora for 1500 dollars and that was our start-up cash.

All that was left to do was to think of a name. We bandied about lots of cute little names—"The Pot Party," "Greenthumbs," "The Plant Orphanage"...and then in a burst of true inspiration, Lynn came up with the name: "Mother Earth, a Plant Boutique".

By ten o'clock that morning, after a freshening shower and a change of clothes, we went out looking for a store to rent. I took the valley, Lynn searched the West Side. At about two o'clock that afternoon, Lynn and I rendezvoused and she was flushed with excitement. "I found the perfect place for Mother Earth" she gushed. "It's on Melrose in West Hollywood, in the back of an arcade. It's a little apartment that can be turned into a store. It has beamed wood ceilings and a fireplace, and the best part is it's only $275 a month!"

I set off to see Lynn's find. It was on Melrose, all right - at least the address was on Melrose, but the room was hidden way in the back of this arcade and invisible from the street. To give you an idea, the address was 8570 and 1/4! Not that it mattered. There was absolutely no walk-by traffic and no place to park, so who was going to come there? And talk about small - how about 600 square feet? Sure, it was homey, and cute, but still...

Lynn would not be discouraged. She was sure it was all going to work. So we set about prepgraring for our grand opening. Within two weeks we had fully outfitted our tiny little store with lots and lots of beautiful plants in funky containers, and had commissioned a tiny little sign to put out front of the arcade. We took beautiful color photographs of the store, had 300 invitations printed up for the opening and sent invitations and photographs to 300 friends and acquaintances.

We rented a searchlight for the opening night, had wine and cheese spread out and, believe it or not, at least 200 people showed up. By the time the party ended we had practically sold out every bit of our merchandise. We were a hit!

At least, so it seemed.

We re-stocked the store and a week later opened up for business. The days passed and nobody came. Almost literally. One or two people a day happened in, having been in the arcade for some other purpose. (Next door to us, unbeknownst to us when we rented the store, was a "massage parlor", wink wink, and the clientele there was not exactly looking for cute little plants.) By the end of the first month, we were becoming desperate. It looked like our dream had died and I was resigned to going back into show-business. I decided to take one last shot.

I sat down and wrote the article I had imagined would launch our success. I titled it "TV Writer Goes from Show-Biz to Grow-Biz" and sent it in to a reporter at the *Los Angeles Times* whose by-line often appeared over similar stories. Three days later I got a call from said reporter—she loved the story and wondered if she might drop by the store with a photographer. Would tomorrow be okay? We were ecstatic. We called several of our friends and assigned each a time to come in and pretend to be a customer, promising we'd refund their money as soon as the reporter left. We had shills lined up from noon until two o'clock. We figured two hours would be more than enough time.

The reporter and photographer came at noon. They left at 4:30. All our shills had come and gone and not one "real" customer had showed up in the interim. But the reporter hardly noticed. She had fallen in love with the store, the concept, us, and promised a story would appear in the near future.

For the next few nights I stopped on the way home at a newsstand which stocked in tomorrow's paper tonight. Nothing. And then one magic night, I opened up the paper and there, on the front page of the Calendar section, was a headline that stretched across the entire bottom half of the paper: "TV Writer Goes from Show-Biz to Grow-Biz" it read, and under it was a two-column picture of me and Lynn standing by our pitiful little sign. The article was continued on page 3, page 4, and finally ended on page 5. My own mother could not have written a better "review."

Never mind that the next morning one of the biggest earthquakes in Los Angeles history struck at 6 a.m. By the time we opened the store at ten o'clock the phone was ringing off the hook. "Where are you located, where are you located, where are you located?" And by 11 o'clock people were swarming up and down the arcade path like an army of ants.

The dream had begun, but it was only just the beginning of a seven-year odyssey that would be filled with the highest of highs and finally, the lowest of lows.

How a Martian Got Me Into Plants

It's probably worth a moment here to tell you how I got interested in houseplants in the first place.

It all began sometime in the late 50s or early 60s when I was pretty highly involved with another set of little green creatures—characters on a television show you might recall named *My Favorite Martian* for which I wrote a couple of scripts. Now if you think *watching* television sitcoms is frustrating, imagine the terrors of having to write it! I still shudder at the memory.

Anyway, one day I was driving home from a particularly nerve-shattering story conference wherein one of the lines in my script had been criticized on that basis that—get this, folks— *"A Martian wouldn't say that,"* and I decided I needed a little nip to clear my head.

I pulled over to the curb, got out of my car, and headed for a flashing sign that said, "Bar" just down the block. But as I headed to the saloon, I happened to walk by what turned out to be a little nursery and I stopped to look through its foggy window. Something told me to open the door and go inside, so I did.

Good God! I had stumbled into paradise! The place was a jungle of beautiful tropical plants! Naturally at this point in my life I didn't know these gorgeous things had scientific names. To me, all plants were either palms or ferns, none of which could live more than an hour in your care unless you had a degree in botany of horticulture. But despite their anonymity, they certainly presented a dazzling array of shapes and colors and sizes. They smelled good, they looked fabulous, and the atmosphere was serene. Incredible, I thought. I've discovered my own Tahiti right here in the center of Hollywood.

I started wandering through this glorious little rainforest, and suddenly, the next thing I knew....I was talking to a plant! There I stood, spilling out the troubles of my day to this poor, innocent, but uncomplaining *Sansevieria laurentii* —I knew it was a Sansevieria—it was wearing a name-tag. What's more, it was listening! Unlike the average bartender who puts up with a trouble-ridden monologue because he wants a bigger tip, this silly looking little plant really cared, I could tell. Being that it was a stiff, multi-stalked plant that looked like it could have been from another planet, I picked it up and told it about the line in my script and asked it: "Do you think a Martian would say that?" and a voice replied, "I beg your pardon?" I almost fainted until I realized it was the nurseryman, who had come into the room behind me.

Properly embarrassed, I picked up the plant, bought it, forgot completely about going to the bar, and took it home where I could continue my monologue. The first thing I did was give it a new name. Tired of calling it Sansevieria laurentii, I named my new friend Irving after a favorite uncle who had a similar sort of imperturbability.

I talked to Irving for another half-hour at least. Then I put him to bed on my dresser and went to bed myself for the first time in months without a sleeping pill. Quite by accident I had discovered the perfect tranquilizer!

Irving thrived , I was hooked on the whole idea that you could actually grow things in your home or apartment, I began buying plants and learning how to care for them, mostly by trial and error, and now here I am, years later, "The World's Foremost Authority on Indoor Gardening".

Only in America!

Never Judge a Book By Its Cover

I took great pride in my sales staff at Mother Earth. When we finally closed shop I had 17 fabulous young people, average age about 23, sharing shifts on the floor, all of them making darned good money for kids of their age. The criteria for becoming a member of the staff at ME were intelligence, neatness, creativity, and a love of the plants. Plus, of course, being a good salesperson. My gang each made an hourly salary, plus a generous 6% of the gross on every sale they made. A job at Mother Earth was a real plum for these kids who were all working their way through some sort of creative schooling, be it art, film, music, whatever. I must have turned down a hundred applicants for every person I hired.

We had all sorts of customers at Mother Earth, about 90% of them just plain ordinary folks—secretaries, nurses, doctors, lawyers, police officers, you name it—and the other 10% were what I would call celebrities: Sally Struthers, Rock Hudson, Robert Montgomery, Michael Douglas, Mama Cass, Lucille Ball, Michele Lee, Vikki Carr, Ruth Buzzi and many others of their ilk. My salespeople, naturally, presumed the celebrities would spend more money, than a "regular person" might spend, and although this was not universally true, the wealthier clientele did tend to spend more than most people. So when a recognizable celebrity came walking down the path, the salespeople would always jockey for position. The rule was, when one of my gang waited on a celebrity, that person would become his or her customer for the duration. In the end, It all worked out fairly for the paychecks were always very close to the same at the end of every week. (Interestingly, some of my wealthiest clients were the ones who haggled about every price while the kids obviously living from paycheck to paycheck never quibbled.)

One day when business was fairly slow a young couple came walking

The Mother Earth creed

down the path toward the store. He was tall and terribly skinny with shoulder-length hair, a drooping mustache and wearing a torn tee-shirt and ripped jeans (before ripped jeans were in fashion.) She was practically anorexic, looked as if she hadn't washed her hair in weeks, and was dressed in virtually the same kind of clothes as her companion. There were about six salespeople available at the time, and when I alerted them to the approaching customers all six of them suddenly scampered to find something to do. "Gotta clean the back windows, boss"... "I've been meaning to replant that terrarium..." Not one of them wanted to waste their precious time waiting on these deadbeats in the event a "real" customer might show up. So the greeting of these two was left to me.

"Hi," the guy said as he reached the store. "My name is Chuck Negron, and this is my wife Paula." The name meant nothing to me, but they were customers so I smiled and welcomed them to Mother Earth. "Is the owner here?" Mr. Negron asked. "I'm the boss," I said. "May I help you?" "I hope so," he said. "My accountant just called and said we had to spend $30,000 dollars by the end of the day or we'll be screwed on our taxes. So we were wondering if somebody could come up and take a look at our house and fill it up with plants."

I looked them up and down and smiled again. "Really?" I said. "What kind of business are you in that you make so much money?" "You ever hear of Three Dog Night?" he asked. Was he kidding? Three Dog Night was one of the biggest rock groups of all time!! "Joy to the World" alone had sold over 12 million copies! I frowned..."So you are...?" "I'm the lead singer," said Chuck. "And I'd like you to come up to the house and fill it up with thirty-thousand dollars worth of plants if you've got the time."

If I had the time? That would be the biggest single installation we'd ever done, next to the one we did for Jennifer Jones and her husband, Norton Simon. Well, you should have seen the look on my salespeople's faces as they raced over to try and wrest the job from me. They knew that Lynn and I rarely had time to do those big installations, and they were suddenly all babbling at once that they'd be happy to take the gig. I guess!

I followed the Negrons and their huge Mercedes-Benz up to a really palatial Mediterranean-style villa in Nichols Canyon, where I spent the next four hours walking around with Paula and turning the house into a replica of Mother Earth. (While Paula and I toured and planted, Chuck tucked himself away in his den where he occupied his time taking every illicit drug known to man—marijuana, cocaine, heroin, you name it. In his book, *Three-Dog Nightmare*, Chuck admitted to all his habits and as this is written has been clean and sober for years.) When I finally couldn't find one more place to put a plant, I showed the estimate to Chuck. "I'm sorry," I said, "But I've practically filled the house to the brim and I still can't get it up to thirty thousand—all I can squeeze out is twenty-two-five." Chuck thought about it for a minute, then went into his den, where the walls were papered with platinum records, and wrote out a check for thirty-thousand bucks.

"Keep the change," he said. "I know it's gonna be worth every penny."

And frankly, it was. By the time we were finished with the job his house was the envy of everyone who walked through his door. Lots of his friends came to Mother Earth and asked for the same treatment, and from then on I parceled the jobs out to my kids.

We all learned a lesson that day: As much as it was a cliche, it was wise to remember that one should never judge a book by its cover. Especially if you're a salesperson working for commission at a retail store.

P.S. I later learned that my father had once done the same thing on purpose: He had let his beard grow out for couple of days, put on some crummy clothes and walked into the local Cadillac dealership with ten grand in his pocket. He was amused by the way the salepeople all avoided him as he walked around the show-room, then had a good laugh when he pulled out the wad of dough and pointed to a snazzy convertible—"I'll take this one," he said, and then he made the salesmen draw straws which he had brought to see who would get the sale. "I know it was kind of mean," he said, "but I hope I taught 'em a lesson." I'm sure he did.

Ruth Buzzi

Laugh-In was a seminal comedy program in the 60s, hosted by a comedy team called Rowan and Martin, and probably best remembered for having introduced Goldie Hawn to the world.

One of the key cast members of that show was a woman named Ruth Buzzi, a terrifically talented comedienne who was, to be gentle, not especially attractive. Her best known character was a frankly ugly old woman who got her laughs by beating fellow cast member Arte Johnson over the head with her purse in what became one of the show's trademark sketches.

Ruth was one of our very first customers, in the days that Mother Earth was struggling to build a clientele, and she and her husband, Bill Keko, became our very good friends. In fact, Ruth was responsible for getting us lots of publicity through her many friends in the various media, and she often came into the store just to visit. She loved the plants, and would eagerly wait on customers during the times she was in the store just hanging around.

Ruth, Bill, Lynn and I had some great times together, but the most memorable was the night of a surprise birthday party Bill gave her in their lovely Hollywood Hills home.

Ruth had lots of celebrity friends—Goldie, Liza Minnelli , and Jack Nicholson were frequent guests at her home for dinner parties, but her one true idol was a dapper, silver-haired gentleman named Robert L. Greene. Robert L., as he was known to his pals, was the fashion editor of Playboy Magazine, and a regular on the talk-show circuit. He was an extraordinary raconteur with an incredibly sharp wit and an almost-British accent that he once described to Johnny Carson as "affected". Ruth thought he was the funniest, most colorful person she had ever seen and heard, and often expressed a wistful desire someday to meet him. (To give you an idea of Robert L.'s personality, he once wrote a book on entertaining, and his instructions on how to give a children's party began by "go out onto your property and rope off a couple of acres.")

Which brings us to the surprise party. While trying to think of an appropriate gift to give a woman who had practically everything—husband Bill had been raised in near poverty and delighted in spending Ruth's money on every gadget that hit the stores—I had an inspiration. I called Robert L., whose home bases were an apartment in Manhattan and a farm in Bucks County, Pennsylvania—and asked him if he'd like to come to Ruth's party. Here was the deal: I would pay his way and put him up for the weekend if he would agree to let me give him to Ruth as a "gift". Robert L., never one to turn down a freebie, jumped at the chance, and arrived in L.A. right on schedule the day of the bash.

I have lost the snapshot of the moment, but I'll never forget the expression on Ruth's face when she opened the door and saw her idol standing there, wrapped from head to toe in cellophane and topped off with a giant blue bow.

It may have been the best gift I ever gave to anybody.

Author, Author!

One morning in late 1972 I got a phone call at Mother Earth from a man named Larry Sloane, a partner in a small Los Angeles book publishing company. Larry was a big fan of the store, had seen Lynn and me many times on television, knew of my writing background, and thought it would be a wonderful idea if we were to write a book on houseplant care.

Having been a television and B-movie writer my entire writing life, the idea of becoming an actual "author" was beguiling. Lynn was as excited about the idea as I was, so I agreed to meet Larry and his editor-in-chief for lunch that very day. We convened at a local restaurant, and Larry was effusive in his praise for what we had accomplished. He was convinced that a best-selling book would put us over the top. It would be the next logical step in an adventure that was headed for the really big, big time, moneywise. He envisioned a book designed for the beginning plant person, written with the sort of humor I had honed over the sitcom years.

After about an hour of ego-bursting romance from both Larry and his editor, I was hooked. I took the plunge and asked Larry how much money we were talking about for writing this book. After all, as much as I wanted to become an author, I was still a businessman and I was curious to know how much dough was involved. "Five hundred dollars is the traditional advance for a book like this," Larry said. "And then, of course, you would get a percentage of everything the book earned over that amount." My enthusiasm suddenly took a serious dip. Five hundred dollars sure didn't sound like enough for me to commit to the time and effort that would be involved in writing the book. "Not to worry," he said. "If the book sells like I think it can—we're talking 25 to 50,000 copies—you'll wind up with a goodly sum and round, I promise." I

THE MILLION-COPY BESTSELLER, REVISED AND UPDATED!

MOTHER EARTH'S HASSLE-FREE INDOOR PLANT BOOK

Lynn Rapp and Joel Rapp

Author of
Mr. Mother Earth's Most Rewarding Houseplants

FAWCETT COLUMBINE 90428/$0.00 in USA • $00.00 in Canada

The classic book for houseplant lovers with busy lives.

took a moment to think it over, and then I told them I was pretty sure it was a deal and I'd call them as soon as I got back to the store and talked it over with Lynn.

Life certainly works in mysterious ways.

As I was walking up the arcade path leading to the store, I saw Lynn standing on the front patio talking to a nice-looking fellow with a preppyish haircut and large, horn-rimmed glasses. I moved up to them and the man turned around and smiled broadly. "Hi," he said. "My name is Jeremy

Tarcher, and I have a book-publishing company up on the Sunset strip."
We shook hands, and Jeremy continued: "Lynn tells me you just had
lunch with Larry Sloane. Did he make you an offer to write a book on
plant care?" I nodded. "Yes, as a matter of fact he did." "Did you accept?"
"Well," I said cautiously, "not exactly. I told him I'd discuss the offer with
Lynn and get back to him this afternoon." "Tell you what," said Jeremy.
"I'll give you twice whatever he offered you if you'll write the book for
me. And you won't be sorry, I promise you." He then launched into what
amounted to a soft sales pitch on why we would be much better off with
his company than with Larry's. I started thinking about it. Although I
had liked Larry and his editor, I had already decided I liked Jeremy better
after only a couple of minutes of conversation. There was something genuine and sincere about him that had been missing at the lunch meeting—
and the fact that he was married to Shari Lewis was a big factor as well.
(Both Lynn and I were big Shari Lewis fans, and Lamb-Chop was one of
our favorite characters.) Jeremy pushed on. "How much did he offer for
an advance?" "Fifteen-hundred dollars," I said, praying that I hadn't just
killed a deal. "Three-thousand it is," said Jeremy, sticking out his hand.
"And 6% royalty moving up to 10% depending upon sales." I looked at
Lynn, she nodded emphatically, and I shook Jeremy's hand. "It's a deal!" I
said, and *Mother Earth's Hassle-Free Indoor Plant Book* was born.

We went to work on the manuscript almost at once, and with Jeremy's
guiding hand shaping things every inch of the way, we produced what we
felt was a perfect beginner's handbook. At Jeremy's suggestion we hired an
illustrator named Marvin Rubin, whose incredible line-drawings added
untold value to the book. Bantam Books called and offered to buy the
paperback rights, which Jeremy sold for fifteen-thousand dollars of which
I think we got half, and things were looking very bright as we approached
our publication date. The first printing was scheduled to be 25,000 copies, and Jeremy was very excited—he was convinced that with proper
promotion the book might sell as many as a hundred-thousand copies
over the long haul. He put his money where his mouth was by hiring a
publicity person especially to put together a book tour for me and Lynn,
and then another Miracle in the parade of Mother Earth Miracles came to
pass:

For several months I had been appearing once a week on *The Dinah
Shore Show*—a half-hour program that aired five-days a week wherein Dinah
and a celebrity guest would learn how to cook, do various crafts, and take care

Lynn & Joel Rapp (Ms. & Mr. Mother Earth)

The authors, who created the original plant boutique called "Mother Earth," have written two previous books, and a nationally syndicated newspaper column, "Dear Mother Earth." They are not botanists, but just ordinary people like us who have conquered all the usual mistakes made in raising houseplants, and want to share their commonsense approach with everyone.

Check out those hairdos!

of their houseplants—my department. One day her guest was the famous insult comedian, Don Rickles, and when Don and Dinah arrived at my "station", hilarity ensued. I was trying to describe how to plant something or another, but Rickles was at his all-time funniest and before the segment was over the studio audience was doubled over with tears of laughter.

After the show, I was approached by a man who looked like he might have been a member of the Mob. He introduced himself as Joe Scandore,

Rickles' manager, and as I noted the deep scar on his forehead and the way he spoke out of the corner of his mouth, I determined my initial impression was probably right on target. "What's with the plants and funny?" he asked. I assured him it was Rickles who had made the segment funny, but Scandore shook his head. "Uh-unh," he said. "It was the two of you together. I like the act, kid, and I'll tell you what I'm gonna do. Next time Don hosts the Tonight Show "- Rickles was one of Johnny Carson's regular fill-in hosts— "I'm gonna have you on." We shook hands and I went back to the store and excitedly told Lynn the good news. "I'll believe it when I see it," she said, and cooler heads prevailed. She was right. We'd believe it when we saw it.

Three weeks later, exactly five days before 25,000 copies of *Mother Earth's Hassle-Free Indoor Plant Book* were due to arrive at bookstores everywhere, we got a call from a producer at *The Tonight Show*. "Don Rickles is hosting the show Wednesday night," she said, "and he's requested that you and your wife come onto the show." I almost fainted with joy and excitement. "We'll be there, we'll be there!" I practically shouted into the phone. "Great," said the producer. "Now what is it exactly that you people do?" "We do plants," I replied, and there was a deafening silence on the other end of the line. "Plants?" the woman finally managed to stammer. "You mean, like…ferns and philodendrons?" "Yep," I said. "You know, the care and feeding of indoor plants." "But we don't do plants on the Tonight Show," she said, nervously. "Oh?" I replied. "Are you going to say no to Joe Scandore?" She laughed. "I get the point," she said, so we sealed the deal and agreed that it being just before Easter we would do a segment on the care and feeding of Easter lilies and a lesson on how to nurture the bulbs into bloom again after the plant expires. "See you Wednesday night," she said. "There'll be a drive-on pass at the gate."

I called Jeremy as soon as I hung up and told him the news. He was ecstatic, to say the least. "Do you know how big a deal this is?" he enthused. "I'm going to call the printer and order another two-hundred thousand copies!"

The big night arrived, and Lynn and I arrived at the NBC gate at the appointed hour. "We're Lynn and Joel Rapp," I said to the guard. "We're going to be guests on The Tonight Show." The guard took out a clipboard and looked it up and down. "Sorry," he said. "I don't see any Lynn and Joel Rapp listed here." My heart sank. What could be wrong.

"But that's impossible," I said. "They said there'd be a drive-on pass. See, we're Mr. and Ms. Mother Earth, and we're supposed to—" The guard cut me off with a smile. "Ah, here it is," he said. "Mr. and Mrs. M. Earth. Go on in, and good luck on the show."

Filled with relief, and laughing about the way we'd been listed on the guard's sheet, we headed into the studio where the producer helped us set up for our demonstration and we rehearsed it a couple of times. We went to our dressing room, where a blue card that said "Mr. and Mrs. M. Earth" was taped onto the door, and waited and paced while the entire butterfly population of the planet Earth swirled in our respective stomachs. Show time finally arrived and we watched on our dressing room monitor while Rickles did his opening monologue and introduced his first guest, Gina Lollobridgida. God, she was beautiful, and when we were finally summoned and informed we were up next, my knees were shaking doubly hard—as many times as we had appeared on TV shows, this one was the biggie, and on top of that I was going to sit next to one of my all time faves, Gina L.

Well, what ensued for the next 20 minutes was pure, unadulterated laughter. Rickles must have held up the book ten times in our first ten-minute segment, and then, after a commercial break, we repaired to our planting table where we attempted to show Don how to plant an Easter Lilly bulb. I wish I could fully describe what went on, but suffice to say I doubt the Tonight Show ever experienced a more hilarious segment—most of it consisting of Rickles making jokes at our expense.

After the show, Scandore came over to us, beaming. He wanted to sign us up and be our manager, which offer we gratefully accepted, and he promised us future guestings on the show. All told we appeared on The Tonight Show eight times—never with Johnny Carson, always with a guest host—but eight times nevertheless on a show that "didn't do plants".

Mother Earth's Hassle-Free Indoor Plant Book got rave reviews, (*The Los Angeles Times* called it "the seminal book on indoor gardening"), went on to sell almost *three-million* copies in various editions, and Lynn and I were now well on our way to that fantastic dream of only four years before—the night we sat with Larry Marks and his wife and predicted someday Mother Earth would be a multi-million dollar enterprise. And Jeremy Tarcher's company burst into the national limelight and became one of the biggest and most successful publishers in the country. In fact, when Jeremy would introduce us to friends of his, he would always add, "These are the people who made my company what it is today." And of course, we would always add, "And vice-versa."

The success of that book led to untold opportunities, among them several more books, a column with the Times-Mirror Syndicate, and contracts for regular appearances with Mike Douglas, Phil Donahue, *The Today Show*, and several others of only slightly lesser rank. But the most rewarding thing about *Mother Earth's Hassle-Free Indoor Plant Book*, other than fostering a life-long friendship with Jeremy, was the fact that it turned on millions of people to the joys of the indoor gardening experience, many thousands of whom wrote to thank us for opening that great green door. For that I am most humbly grateful.

The Man Who Loved Bromeliads

Here's a little quiz for you film buffs: What do the following movies have in common: *The African Queen, The Maltese Falcon, Key Largo, Prizzi's Honor, Annie, Night of the Iguana, The Misfits, Heaven Knows, Mr. Allison, Moby Dick, Beat the Devil, Moulin Rouge, The Red Badge of Courage, The Asphalt Jungle,* and *The Treasure of Sierra Madre?*

Yes, all of them are fabulous, even classic films, but more importantly, all were directed by the great John Huston.

Being the movie lover that I am, John Huston was always one of my idols, so imagine the thrill that swept over me when I walked into the "Jungle Room" at Mother Earth one morning to find The Great Man himself sitting on an overturned flower-pot, listening to the burbling of the waterfall and taking in the rich, humid atmosphere. The "Jungle Room" was my favorite room among all the many rooms that made up Mother Earth—that's where the exotic plants were kept: The orchids, the delicate ferns, the flowering things, and the bromeliads. For the uninitiated, bromeliads are a family of plants which are known as "epiphytes", plants that grow on a host but unlike parasites, do not live off it, taking their nourishment from the air. There are hundreds of species and thousands of varieties, and all produce gorgeous, spear-like blooms. There are clubs all over the world dedicated to the care and study of bromeliads, populated by dedicated folks who really love these particular plants. Turns out that Mr. Huston was one of those folks.

I introduced myself to the esteemed director and gushed about my admiration for his work. He, in turn, thanked me for the compliment, and then paid me one in return: "This is one of the best collections of bromeliads I've ever seen," he said. "You really are to be congratulated. It's clear from your store that you really love the plants." Talk about making my day! How about my year??

Of course I wanted to spend whatever time he'd give me to talk about his legendary film career, but Mr. Huston only wanted to talk about the plants. He described his own love of bromeliads to me in detail, and related stories of having gone on treks to South America and Mexico looking for specific specimens to add to his collection.

He stayed and talked with me for over an hour and picked out several plants to buy. But I wasn't going to let him leave without giving him a special gift: I had a truly magnificent stag-horn fern hidden away in the back of the store that I had raised from a pup and which was not for sale, and while he was paying for his purchases I retrieved the extraordinary specimen—it had a "wingspan" of almost six feet across—and gave it to him as a gift. He tried to refuse it, knowing how much it meant to me, but I convinced him that it was the least I could do, given how much pleasure his movies had brought to me over the years.

He never came back to the store, at least as far as I knew, but I got a card from him about a year later telling me the staghorn was thriving and had produced a bunch of "pups".

It was that kind of joy that made the Mother Earth experience so wonderfully unique.

I Loved Lucy
(And better yet, she loved me!)

Of all the celebrity clients who frequented Mother Earth, my favorite, far and away, was Lucille Ball.

Ironically, I had first met Lucy when I was one of many writers on one of her latter-day shows, titled, eponomously, *The Lucy Show*—the one where she worked in a bank managed by her old sidekick Gale Gordon. During those days, when I was a mere writer, she hardly paid me any notice, and believe me, I understood.

But many years later, when she became a regular customer at Mother Earth and I took on the role of her official "plant man", we became the best of friends.

Although she had a heart of gold, Lucy was one of the cheapest people I have ever known. I remember when she first came into the store and after looking around for awhile she said, "I'll take this, and this, and this. How much?" I told her, and she almost fainted dead away. "What??" she practically screamed. "Who do you think I am, Princess Grace??" I couldn't help but laugh and shake my head, and even though I never gave *anybody* a discount, I heard myself saying "Okay. For you I'll take 10% off. But please, don't tell anybody. I don't want to get a reputation for being a pushover." She hugged me and promised she'd keep our secret—and she did.

Her daughter, Desiree, AKA "Little Lucy", was a customer as well. Unlike her mom, she never complained about the prices and she became a close, personal friend of mine as well. One day she called up from somewhere back east where she was appearing in a show. It was Mama's birthday, and she wanted me to send her a gift. "How much do you want to spend?" I asked. "Up to fifty dollars," she replied. "And be sure to send something really nice." I assured her I would and hung up, knowing ex-

111

actly what I would send over to Lucy. That week I'd gotten in a shipment of really huge, exquisite Boston ferns, priced at $75, a bargain at that. Lucy, who had a beautiful home in Beverly Hills with a spacious back-yard, had admired the ferns and commented that one of them would be beautiful on her patio. For whatever reason, she failed to add a fern to her purchase, so I decided that one of those beauties would be the perfect gift.

I put a large bow around the hanger, discounted the price for Desiree down to $50, and sent it over to Lucy's house. About an hour later my phone rang. It was Lucy. "I just got that fern," she said. I could tell from her tone she was angry. "Don't you love it?," I asked. "Of course I love it," she replied. "But how dare you sell Desiree a $75 plant? You know she can't afford that kind of money!" I sighed. "Lucy," I said, "I know she's a struggling young actress, so I only charged her fifty. Okay?" There was a pause, and then in a much softer voice she said. "Oh. That was very sweet of you. I'll send you the extra twenty-five." Of course, I refused, and a bit later I sent along a companion fern as a gift from all of us at Mother Earth.

Does anyone remember when Lucy starred in a movie remake of *Auntie Mame*? It was around the same time I was hosting a radio talk-show at KFI in Los Angeles. Well during the shooting of that movie she had a skiing accent and had broken her leg, forcing her to work with a cast all the way up to her knee. During this period, her "man", Eddie, came by the store with a large, domed, plastic terrarium. He said that Lucy wanted me to plant it up, and she needed to know how much it would cost. I knew at once that we were talking a lot of money, and knowing Lucy I figured she'd rebel. So I told Eddie I'd make her a deal: "Tell her if she'll come on my radio program for an hour I'll do it for free." I could hardly believe it when she called me a little bit later. "I'll come and do it," she said, "but it's blackmail!" Three days later she hobbled into the studio during a precious break from filming and spent an hour gabbing with me and taking phone calls from delirious listeners. That was the day I got the notion that Lucy cared for me maybe as much as I cared for her. Cheap as she was, she would never have gone to all that trouble just to save a few bucks on a terrarium.

My suspicions of her affection were confirmed one hot summer day many years later in New York, where I had moved after the demise of Mother Earth. I was walking down a street in Greenwich Village when I saw what was obviously a movie company at work in the blazing sun. As I got closer, I saw what appeared to be an old bag lady sitting in a chair reading a script. A huge circle of people were gathered around several yards away. I reached the circle and saw that the "bag lady" was Lucy, in costume for a TV movie she was shooting.

I walked over to one of the guards and told him I'd like to speak to Miss Ball, and he shook his head. "She's busy studying lines," he said. "She can't talk to anybody." "Tell her it's Mr. Mother Earth," I said, and the guard shrugged and walked over to Lucy. She listened for a moment, then leaped out of the chair and came running over and enfolded me in an embrace. "How are you," she gushed. "Are you all right?" She held me at arms length and looked me up and down. "Are you eating right? Taking care of yourself?" She'd heard about my divorce and was obviously concerned. I assured her all was well. And to prove I was eating right, I invited her to join me for dinner that night. She accepted, and we had a lovely dinner at a local restaurant. And at her insistence, she picked up the tab.

The last time I saw Lucy was a morning a few years later. I had moved back to L.A. with my new wife, Suzie, and the phone rang early one Saturday morning. It was Lucy. I had stopped by her house a few days earlier and dropped off a few little miniature African violets as a "just because" gift, and she was calling to ask where she could go and get some to take to her friend Ruth Berle, who was gravely ill in nearby Cedars-Sinai hospital. "I'll go pick some up for you," I said, and she got indignant. "I can go myself," she said. "I'm not a cripple!" "That's okay," I told her, "I was going over to that nursery anyway." So I brought her the violets, we visited for a few minutes in her backyard over ice tea, and then I left.

The very next week Lucy herself entered Cedars-Sinai and soon after she passed away.

She was, truly, one of a kind, and I shall never, ever forget her.

Wolfgang—
And I Don't Mean Mozart

I guess almost everybody knows the name Wolfgang Puck—America's Number One celebrity chef, proprietor of a string of upscale restaurants, and the man who took frozen pizza to new and spectacular heights.

He could never have done it without me.

One day, a tall, handsome young man came into the store, accompanied by a small, not-so-handsome companion. The taller man introduced himself. "My name is Patrick Terrail," he said, "And I'm about to open a new restaurant called Ma Maison down the block from here. And this," he pointed proudly at his friend, "is my chef, Wolfgang Puck." We shook hands all around, and I asked Patrick what I could do for him.

"I'd like you to come over and fill up my restaurant with plants," he said, "both inside and outside on my patio. How about it?"

I told him I'd be delighted to come down and look the space over and give him an estimate, and it was then he raised his hand and made a proposition. "I haven't got a lot of cash right now," he admitted, "but I'll make you a deal. I'll trade you the plants for meals—straight up, retail for retail."

I hesitated. "Hmmm," I said. "Restaurants are very hazardous ventures," I said. "I don't want to seem negative, but most fancy eateries close fairly quickly here in L.A."

"Ahh, quite true." replied Patrick, putting an arm around Wolfgang's shoulder. "But they don't have Wolfgang Puck for a chef. He's a fabulous cook and once the word gets out people will flock to our restaurant! Believe me—someday Wolfgang will be the most famous chef in the world!"

I was still dubious, so Patrick continued. "Tell you what. Why don't you come down with us, check out the place, and while you're doing your estimate, Wolfgang will cook you lunch? Then you can make up your mind."

I had nothing to lose and a free lunch to gain, so I eagerly accepted. We walked down Melrose to the home of Ma Maison, and while Patrick and I walked around the premises, plotting a planting scheme, Wolfgang retired to the kitchen.

About an hour later I had finished my plan and my estimate. "It's a rather big job," I told Patrick. "Including planters and my usual fee the total comes to $3500. That's an awful lot of meals."

As Patrick pondered the situation, Wolfgang emerged from the kitchen with a steaming plate of food. It was a halibut filet atop a mound of julienned vegetables floating in the most unbelievably delicious sauce I had ever tasted in my life. I nodded. "This is sensational," I said, as Patrick and Wolfgang beamed. "We've got a deal!"

So I put in the plants and began eating regularly at Ma Maison. I went for lunch, Lynn and I went for dinners. We took friends and business associates, and never had anything but a first-class meal. In the beginning, business at the restaurant was typically slow, so there was never a problem getting seated immediately when we arrived. Slowly but surely, we were eating away the debt, which after a couple of months was down to about fifteen-hundred dollars.

Then one day I ambled down the block, hungry for lunch, and was surprised to see the place was packed. A local food critic had, that morning, given Ma Maison a rave review, and Patrick was bustling about trying to keep all the patrons happy.

"Well," I said, when he finally found a moment to come over and greet me. "Looks like things have finally picked up." He smiled broadly. "At last," he said, then, with a little shrug: "I'm sorry, but there'll be about a half-an-hour wait."

That did it. I was happy for Patrick and Wolfgang, but I realized the comfort of dropping into Ma Maison for a casual meal was over. I asked Patrick if he thought he could settle the balance of his bill for cash, and he promised payment within the month.

I got the check, the restaurant flourished, and Wolfgang went on to make Patrick's prediction come true.

As I said—Wolfgang could never have done it without me.

The Death of Mother Earth

During the next seven years, Mother Earth fulfilled every fantasy Lynn and I had ever had, and then some. We expanded, room by room, from the one tiny apartment at the back of the arcade to the entire complex—all four apartments in the back, two storefronts on either side of the arcade, and both storefronts up at the front. We even had a big, beautiful sign on top of the building, just like the one we'd envisioned seven years before.

Our sales went from virtually zero to over a million dollars a year. We grew from one employee to seventeen full time salespeople and several more in our office staff. We became the Tiffany of plant shops; a gift from Mother Earth was as much a status symbol as a Gucci bag. Lynn and I were ubiquitous on radio and television and were recognized on the streets wherever we went. We opened up a Product Development division after one night at a party Vidal Sassoon, the famed hairdresser, reminded us that a line of products was the way to make really serious money—much of it while you slept. We rubbed elbows with and made friends with dozens of famous people and thousands of ordinary folks, all of whom were equals under the roof of Mother Earth. We conducted Plant Care Classes at the store—three classes a day, five days a week—classes that brought over 300 students to the store every week, each one a virtual captive customer. We authored best-selling books and were in constant demand to lecture at high-paying Home and Garden Shows all over the country. And on and on and on. The money was rolling in and Lynn and I were famous. As far as I was concerned, things could not have been rosier. There was no place to go but up.

At least that's what I thought.

Someone once said that "all good things must come to an end," but

117

I'd have bet a lot of money that Mother Earth would last forever. Alas, it was not to be.

The end came in late summer of 1977 when I arrived home from the store one night and Lynn announced, "I'm leaving." "Oh," I replied. "What time will you be back?" "No," she said, "I mean I'm leaving — I'm giving up my role as Ms. Mother Earth and my life as Mrs. Joel Rapp and going off with my friend Bobbie to join the Divine Light Mission of the Guru Maraji."

I was stunned. At first I thought she was joking. This couldn't possibly be happening. Things had never been better at the store, our books were selling like crazy, we had a syndicated plant-care column in over 200 papers, and most importantly we were only a few weeks away from launching the Mother Earth Product Line, the pot of gold at the end of the Mother Earth rainbow in which we had invested over a million dollars of our own hard-earned money.

"You can't be serious," I finally managed to whisper. "I mean, I don't understand…What's going on here?"

Lynn calmly and patiently explained: For the past year she had been quietly having a nervous breakdown. The frantic pace of the business, the constant traveling, the fact that her 15-year-old daughter had felt so neglected she'd run off and gotten pregnant—all of that had taken its toll and she had decided to chuck the whole thing for the peace of mind she felt she would find with the Guru.

Guru Maraji was a 15-year-old boy from India whose father had been a prominent figure in his native land. Upon the death of the elder Guru, the younger Maraji decided to pack his bags and bring his act to America where the simple arithmetic showed there were a lot more dollars to be made in the U.S. than were rupees in India. (If I sound bitter and cynical, I was.) I'll never forget the day in 1970 that Lynn and I were surfing the TV and came across a program being broadcast from the Astrodome in Texas. Fifty-thousand people had gathered in the stadium to hear the teenage guru speak of his "Divine Light Mission" and finding "The Knowledge" therein, and the cheers were deafening as the crowd pledged their love and everlasting devotion. We watched this sideshow fascinated, not knowing whether to laugh or cry at the absurdity of it all. Was the world really that screwed up that tens of thousands of people would actually seek sanctuary in the arms of a teen-age kid?? And had over all their worldly goods in the process? It was the epitome of a Cult, pure and simple.

I wasn't laughing now. Lynn was dead serious. Without my knowledge, she and Bobbie had gone to a few gatherings of the Mission, and somehow had been hypnotized into becoming "devotees". I begged her to reconsider. We had a big house, and as far as I was concerned she and Bobbie were welcome to share a room and go see the guru as often as they felt the need. I cried, I screamed, I raged, but all to no avail. Her mind was made up. She calmly described to me the ways the guru worked: "It's a four-fold process," she intoned. "When the guru holds your temples, there's a blinding light and you see God with your 'third eye'; When he presses your ears you hear the celestial music of God with your 'third ear'; when he puts his finger into your throat you taste the divine nectar of God, and after severe hyperventilation, when you are almost unconscious, you sense the healing vibrations of God".

I was speechless. She actually believed this stuff. She swore to me she had already tasted the nectar, heard the music, and seen the light—and in time she would be rewarded with The Knowledge, whatever that was. Again I implored her at least to stay and continue her duties as Ms. Mother Earth even if our personal relationship came to an end. Our entire business depended upon us being together, like George and Gracie, or Sonny and Cher. The store, the products, the books, the column—since we had no money for advertising and promotion, none of these could possibly sustain without us constantly being out on the road making appearances on radio and television. Our product distributor had already sold several million dollars worth of Mother Earth Plant Food, spray bottles, gardening tool sets—all predicated on our promise to the retailers of continuing constant media publicity.

Lynn was having none of it. As far as she was concerned Mother Earth was a closed chapter in the book of her life. She was going off to the guru with Bobbie and nothing I could say or do could possibly change her mind.

My wife was leaving me for God and another woman. There wasn't really a whole lot I could do. Distraught—I was still in love with Lynn besides being a pragmatist about the store and the products and all that money going down the drain—I fell into a complete depression. I gave the news to my 17 loyal employees at the store and told them to sell all the merchandise and split up the proceeds. I called our distributor and told him to cancel the product orders since I couldn't possibly continue on alone. He begged me to give it a try—why couldn't Mr. Mother Earth just become a solo act? I had thought about it long and hard and decided I just couldn't go it alone. And as far as money was concerned, I called my lawyer and our accountant and learned that after all the debts were taken care of and all the bills paid off, there would be somewhere around a hundred- thousand dollars left in the kitty. Thankfully, Lynn was as good as her word about giving up material things—all she wanted was ten thousand dollars and a few items from the house.

Lynn left and began her new life—she changed her name to Loretta Darling—and I fell apart completely. Feeling sorrier for myself than I had ever believed possible, I awoke every day with the question, "Why me?" on my lips. I moved into a small Beverly Hills apartment, and in spite of the fact my then teen-aged daughter Lisa had moved in with me I began doing drugs at an alarming rate. Marijuana, cocaine, quaaludes, uppers, downers—I was a real basket case, hardly ever leaving the sanctuary of my bedroom except to take Lisa to school in the morning and pick her up in the afternoon. It didn't take long for the hundred grand to disappear, and one day about a year-and-a-half later I found myself broke once again.

I was desperate, to put it mildly. Besides myself, I had two kids to support, not to mention a drug habit. The biggest problem was I didn't know what kind of work I was out of. Was I a gardening expert, a comedy writer, a publicity maven—I didn't have a clue where to turn. Obviously, the drug habit had to go, but what was I to do about an income?

And then I had an inspiration that not only rescued me, but opened up an entire new chapter in the book of *my* life.

All was not lost after all.

Born Again!

It was 1979 and I was at the lowest ebb of my life. I had to stand on my tiptoes to reach the bottom of the barrel. It had been almost two years since Lynn—I mean, Loretta—had gone off with Bonnie and the guru, and the money I'd salvaged from Mother Earth was just about gone. I had reached a point where I had to make *some* kind of move, even if it meant taking a minimum wage job flipping hamburgers or selling ties in a department store.

But that, I decided, would be my last resort. I was a writer, and I was determined that I would write my way out of the morass of self-pity in which I found myself wallowing. After all, I had had a long and illustrious career as a TV writer and book author behind me, and surely I could conjure up something I could sell. I made a few calls to the sitcom producers whom I knew from before the Mother Earth years, but I quickly discovered I had become irrelevant in show-business. A couple of people were willing to let me come in and pitch ideas, but those meetings turned out to be fool's errands.

And then, in a moment of inspiration almost equal to the inspiration which created Mother Earth that nine-year-eternity ago, the idea that would save me struck like a bolt from the blue: I would write a proposal for a book called *Mother Earth's Hassle-Free Vegetable Cookbook*, using the same formula that had worked so well for *Mother's Earth's Hassle-Free Indoor Plant Book*! For many years I had been cooking vegetarian cuisine, I had compiled a treasure trove of fabulous recipes, and although I was not a graduate of Cordon Bleu I had learned to cook by trial and error and become a really good amateur chef.

I tossed away all the drugs except pot, which I felt then and still feel today is far more harmless than liquor, nicotine, or any other drug, and

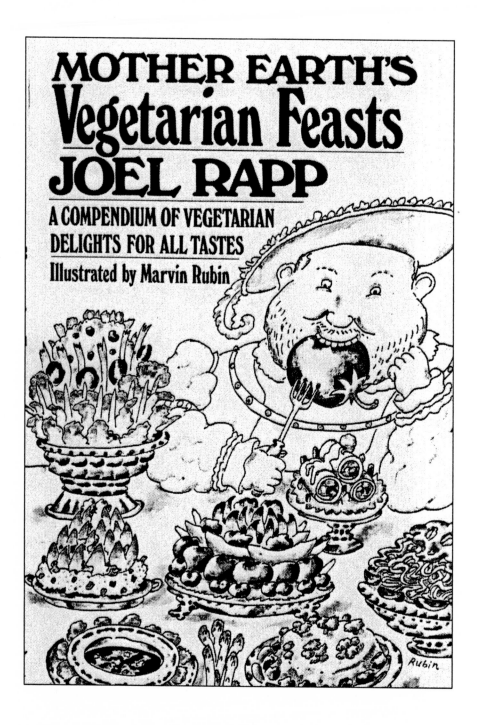

set to work on the cookbook proposal. I wrote a lengthy foreword
explaining the basic aim of the
book, a couple of sample chap-
ters, and then added several of
my favorite recipes. I finished the
proposal in less than two days,
and rushed it over to my dear
friend and publisher, Jeremy
Tarcher. Jeremy, bless him, read
it, thought it was terrific, but
simply didn't buy the idea that
Mr. Mother Earth, the World's
Foremost Authority on Indoor
Gardening, would cut it as a
cookbook author. In spite of the
fact he knew I was in desperate
financial straits, Jeremy reluc-
tantly passed on the proposal.

The truth was that J.P. Tarcher, Inc. was a book publisher, not a charity.

I was devastated. I tried my best to convince Jeremy the book would
be a solid hit, but this was the man who had turned down the first novel
written by his own sister, Judith Krantz, a little number called "Princess
Daisy" which had gone on to sell several million copies, so I was determined not to give it up just because he didn't buy it.

The biggest problem was that I lived in Los Angeles and about 95%
of all publishing was done out of New York. And on top of that, I didn't
have an agent, a critical factor when it comes to selling a book. Some of
my early enthusiasm was beginning to wane, and the old depression was
starting up again, when a couple of nights later I was watching *60 Minutes* and another opportunity roundly knocked. The second segment of
the program was a story about "vanity publishing" wherein authors pay
certain companies to publish their books, and in the body of the segment
they interviewed a man whom they identified as Scott Meredith, "one of
New York's top book agents."

The next morning I got Scott Meredith's number from New York
information and put in a call. I was connected to a man named Jack Scovil,
and the conversation went something like this:

"Hi, Jack. I'll bet you've gotten dozens of calls today from authors looking for representation, right?" "More like hundreds." "Well, my name is Joel Rapp, and you can count me among those authors." There was a pause, and then came some of the sweetest words I have ever heard: "Joel Rapp? Author of "Mother Earth's Hassle-Free Indoor Plant Book?" "That's me," I said. "Wow," Jack said, "what a pleasure to speak to you. I'm one of your biggest fans. What can I do for you?" "I've written a proposal," I said, "and perhaps you can sell it for me." "What's it called?" he asked. I told him, and there was a slightly puzzled pause. "A cookbook?" he said. "I would have thought it was something to do with plants…" "Well," I said, "It's a change of pace, alright, but I have a hunch you'll like what I've written." "Well by all means, send it to me right away," he said, "and I'll get back to you as soon as I've read it. But be thinking about writing a plant book in the meantime, okay?" "Okay," I said, and I hung up, surging with a new wave of optimism.

I mailed the proposal that very morning—that was before e-mail and fax machines—and three days later Jack Scovil called. "I love it," he said. "I'm sure I can sell it!" I looked heavenward — maybe there really was a God! "That's great, Jack, because I'm desperate for cash. Do you think you can sell it quickly?" "Well," he said, "I'm going to send it out tomorrow to 20 publishers and ask them to have a yes or no for me two weeks from Friday. And meantime," he repeated from our earlier conversation, "be working on a plant book, okay?"

The next two weeks felt more like a lifetime. On the day when bids were supposed to come in I was a total nervous wreck. Pacing the floor, waiting for the phone to ring, praying for an offer, any offer.....At about noon the phone finally rang. It was Jack. "I've got great news," he said. "Out of twenty submissions, I've got nineteen offers!" I almost swooned with relief. Then I frowned. "Who didn't offer?" was my first response, and then reality kicked in. "Only kidding," I said. "How much money are we talking, Jack?" "I've got offers from as low as $3500 all the up to $17,500," he said, and I immediately responded, "Well, I guess there really isn't much to discuss. We take the seventeen-five, correct?" "Well, the highest offer isn't always the best offer," he said, "but in this case I'd advise we take it. It's from Avon Books and the editor is named Page Cuddy. She's one of the best editors in the business, and I think you two will get along just great." (Little did he know.) "This is fabulous news, Jack," I said. "But do you think maybe we can pump Ms. Cuddy up to twenty grand?" "Not a chance," he replied. "I already got her up from fifteen. I'm afraid seventeen-five is as high as she'll go." He gave me Page's number and suggested I call and get acquainted with her which I agreed was a good idea. We spoke for a few more minutes, I thanked him profusely for all he had done, and he hung up with a promise of contracts and an advance of half the money within the next couple of weeks.

No sooner had I hung up from Jack than I called Page Cuddy at Avon. "Hi, Page," I said brightly. "This is Joel Rapp calling, and I've got good news and bad news." "Oh?" she said. "And what might that be?" "Well, the good news is you've bought yourself a cookbook and I'm absolutely thrilled. The bad news is it's going to cost you a tad more than you had in mind." "Oh?" she said again. "And how much more would that be?" "Well," I said, "I'd like to get twenty-thousand if you can see your way clear. I really, really need that extra money." There was a somewhat long, thoughtful pause, and then: "Okay. Done." Jack had been right. Page Cuddy and I *were* going to get along great.

After a couple of months of telephone conferences about the book, Page made a trip to Los Angeles and we finally met face to face. There was an instant attraction between us, and a few days later Page convinced me that it would be a much-needed change for me if I picked up and moved to New York. She had a big, beautiful apartment in the West Village and invited me to come live with her. At least give it a try. She even offered to buy me a round-trip ticket, so I had very little, if anything, to lose. By that time Lisa had graduated from high-school and was already out on her own, and Danielle was safely ensconced with her mother. What the hell, I figured. I hated leaving my family behind, and I had no friends in New York, but I truly felt the move would re-invigorate my life. So move I did.

Once in New York we went to work on the cookbook in earnest. We enlisted Marvin Rubin again to contribute his fantastic illustrations, and "Mother Earth's Hassle-Free Vegetable Cookbook" was published about eight months later to great reviews and a sale to the Quality Paperback Book Club as a Main Selection. What a coup! Thanks to the bookclub sale and the good reviews, the book wound up selling almost 400,000 copies and led to two more very successful cookbooks.

My relationship with Page lasted for almost five years, after which we parted, but to this day still remain very close. During my ten-year stay in Manhattan I made a host of wonderful new friends, became a well-known figure on New York radio and television, and completely resurrected by career.

Mr. Mother Earth was born again—this time for keeps.

New York, New York, It's a Wonderful Town

December 24, 1979—the day I arrived in New York to take up residence with Page Cuddy and try to begin a brand new life.

It had been very difficult for me to leave my family in Los Angeles—my daughter Danielle was only 15 and Lisa was barely 19—but they both understood that Dad desperately needed a change of scenery and the move would eventually benefit us all. My mother and father were non-committal as I recall—my mother had already begun to show the symptoms of Alzheimer's Disease which would eventually claim her life, and Dad, sadly, had lost most of his friends and was going through a period of feeling very sorry for himself. ("Why don't you go over to the Club, Dad?" "What for? Everybody's dead.") My brother Paul was my biggest booster (especially when he learned he was going to be the beneficiary of most of my worldly household goods) but he was sincere when he convinced me not to feel guilty—it's a great move, he said, and it will definitely change you life.

And brother, did it ever!

Frankly, although I was literally a native New Yorker, having been born in Sydenham Hospital in Manhattan, I had developed a rather intense dislike for the city. For the past several years, Lynn and I had been making regular monthly trips into Gotham to do our usual round of talk shows, but I admit I was not a big New York fan. The noise, the weather, the crowds, the carelessness—not exactly the life-style a boy from Beverly Hills was used to. But when I arrived for what was basically a trial period that day in 1979, I was determined to make a go of things—my basic goals were to resurrect my career as "Mr. Mother Earth," get a steady job on the radio and TV, and make some good and close friends in the process.

In spite of the fact it was snowing and the temperature was about 20 degrees on the day I arrived, I was much relieved when I walked into Page's

127

apartment. The place, especially for New York, was really quite grand. The apartment was the bottom two-floors of a beautiful four-story 19th century house on Perry Street in the Village. As for our two floors, upstairs there was an enormous living room with a working fireplace, a large dining room, a kitchen that overlooked an enormous back yard (!), and downstairs were two spacious bedrooms and two full baths. Our bedroom, which had been the kitchen when the house had originally been built, featured a huge stone fireplace where the cooking had been done way back when the house was originally built and a back-door that led out into our backyard, which was huge by New York standards and filled with beautiful plants and trees. I certainly had no complaints about the lodgings!

Despite the fact that Lynn and I had been in and out of the city dozens of times, I had no friends there at all, just lots of acquaintances who were on the staffs of the various radio and TV shows that we did when we were in town. Paul Noble, a producer at one of the local TV stations where we made a monthly appearance, was an acquaintance who would turn into a lifelong friend, but for the first few weeks I was really, really lonely and homesick. Page left every morning around 6:30 to go to work and didn't usually get home before 7 or 8 in the evening, so I spent my days wandering the streets of the village, uptown, downtown, the east side and the west side, getting to know my new home town. As far as any social life was concerned, I was Page's partner and her social life was mine. The problem was, frankly, most of her friends were in the publishing business and as far as I was concerned they were way too cold and snobbish for me. And just as frankly, they treated me as if I were a country bumpkin and believe me, I wasn't having any fun. (Interesting about that "bumpkin" thing — turns out I really *was* a bumpkin compared to many middle-class New Yorkers — I thought I was very smart and worldly wise when I first blew into town — but it turned out I was really terribly unsophisticated. During my ten-year tenure in Manhattan I came to be a gourmet, a balletophile, a member of several museums, and even learned to do the *New York Times* Crossword Puzzle—with a pen!)

Anyhow, I'd been in New York about two months and I was still friendless and jobless, a bad combination in any city, to be sure, and especially tough when one is 3000 miles from home and hearth. Several times I threatened to use that ticket back home that I still had crumpled up in my suitcase someplace, driving Page to angrily shout, "Go, stay, but make up your mind already!" Luckily, just in time, something happened that made the decision for me and really turned things around.

Page, my friend and editor

I'd been on the radio in L.A. on several talk-stations as "Mr. Mother Earth", dispensing indoor gardening advice, and decided I'd take a shot at one of the New York stations and see if I could get a gig and start making my comeback. A little sleuthing revealed that two stations in the city carried gardening advice: A fellow named Ralph Snodsmith had held forth on WOR for decades so I wasn't about to try to uproot him— but the woman on WMCA sounded like she could be replaced, so I summoned up those "guts of a policeman" that my father always attributed to me and cold-called the Program Director of the station. His name was Mark Mason, and that phone call began a really memorable personal and business relationship that lasted until I left New York and still exists today.

I gave Mark about two minutes of my best and most winning chatter, and then I jumped to the point: "Is that woman who does your gardening program under contract?" "No," he replied, "she's just here week to week." "Well," I said, "why don't you call her and ask her not to come in this week and give *me* a listen instead? I think you'll be very pleasantly surprised to hear that somebody can actually make a boring subject like gardening into genuine entertainment."

Well, my *chutzpah* plus my sales-pitch had won me the first round— Mark agreed to the plan, but cautioned me that the upcoming Saturday morning gig was strictly an audition. Then I *really* pushed the envelope: "Consider it an audition to host your morning drive show," I said, and he

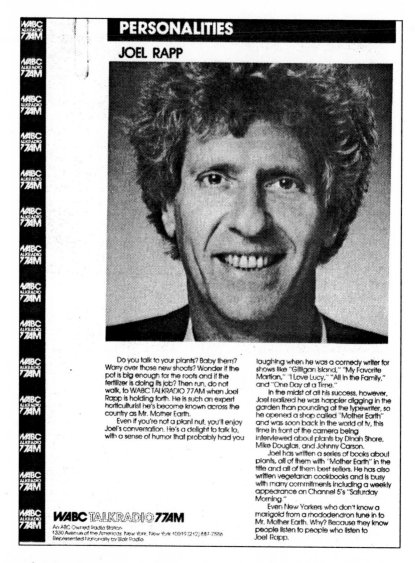

PERSONALITIES

JOEL RAPP

Do you talk to your plants? Baby them? Worry over those new shoots? Wonder if the pot is big enough for the roots and if the fertilizer is doing its job? Then run, do not walk, to WABC TALKRADIO 77AM when Joel Rapp is holding forth. He is such an expert horticulturist he's become known across the country as Mr. Mother Earth.

Even if you're not a plant nut, you'll enjoy Joel's conversation. He's a delight to talk to, with a sense of humor that probably had you laughing when he was a comedy writer for shows like "Gilligan Island," "My Favorite Martian," "I Love Lucy," "All in the Family," and "One Day at a Time."

In the midst of all his success, however, Joel realized he was happier digging in the garden than pounding at the typewriter, so he opened a shop called "Mother Earth" and was soon back in the world of tv, this time in front of the camera being interviewed about plants by Dinah Shore, Mike Douglas, and Johnny Carson.

Joel has written a series of books about plants, all of them with "Mother Earth" in the title and all of them best sellers. He has also written vegetarian cookbooks and is busy with many commitments including a weekly appearance on Channel 5's "Saturday Morning."

Even New Yorkers who don't know a marigold from a rhododendron tune in to Mr. Mother Earth. Why? Because they know people listen to people who listen to Joel Rapp.

WABC TALKRADIO 77AM
An ABC Owned Radio Station
1330 Avenue of the Americas, New York, New York 10019 (212) 887-7586
Represented Nationally by Blair Radio

gasped. Morning Drive is the primest time on the radio and the hosts of those morning shows make the really big bucks—Howard Stern, Rick Dees, the Grambling dynasty, my own daughter Lisa who co-hosts the morning show on KEARTH 101 in Los Angeles. "Why don't we just take it one step at a time," he suggested politely, most likely stifling a laugh. "Okay," I said. "See you on Saturday."

The gardening show at WMCA back in 1980 was on from noon to two Saturday afternoons. I showed up for my "audition" show at about 11, learned which microphone was which and a few other little technicalities, and was pronounced by my producer and engineer that I was good to go. I admit my heart was pounding and my palms were sweating as the clock approached twelve o'clock, but once that red light went on I was fine. I began the program with my signature opening: "Hi there, Philodendron fans!"—and my New York radio career was underway.

Sometime before one o'clock, during a fairly lengthy commercial break, Mark Mason called me in the studio and told me he'd been listening, and by God I had been right—gardening can be entertaining!—and would I be available to sit in all next week for the vacationing Candy Jones? I contained my joy and coolly accepted, and then added: "But don't forget about that morning drive slot…" The following Monday night I came to work in place of a New York radio legend, Candy Jones, outside my usual gardening format. This time, Mark had a chance to hear Joel Rapp instead of "Mr. Mother Earth." Joel Rapp, I explained to him, was who I wanted to wind up on morning drive. This time he didn't laugh at all.

I spent the next three years at WMCA, alternating between my weekend shows on gardening which had been expanded to Sundays as well and acting as the station's designated "pinch hitter"—anytime anybody was sick or on vacation, I sat in their place. I sat in at every conceivable time-slot—mornings, afternoons, evenings—for some of the biggest names in the history of New York radio: Barry Gray, Barry Farber, Long John Neibold, Bob Grant, Sally Jesse Raphael…I filled in seamlessly for the best talkers in the biz. (Remember back in high school I was voted "Most Loquacious"? Well, it finally paid off!) But when a full-time gig would open up every now and then, I couldn't convince Mark to give me the job. "You're too valuable to me as a pinch-hitter," he'd say with a logic I still feel is flawed to say the least, and I continued to shlep along in my less than starring role. But the benefits from being on the radio were enormous. I was in constant demand for lectures, home shows, TV appearances, you name it.

Then one day in 1983 things changed: Mark Mason applied for and won the coveted job as Program Director at WABC, at that time the highest rated talk show station in America in the biggest radio market in the world . He asked me to come along—I'd have to play "Mr. Mother Earth" in the beginning, but he'd see to it that things would all work out. So I followed Mark to WABC as soon as my contract with WMCA ended two months later, and the next three years were almost identical to my three years at WMCA—except I was getting paid twice as much. Actually, I was more than satisfied with the arrangement. I had my regular gardening show every weekend which kept all the important doors wide open for Mr. Mother Earth, and I also had lots of sit-in work for other general-interest programs which was earned me psychic satisfaction and lots of extra money.

It was at the station's Christmas Party in 1986 that Mark Mason finally made his move. He sidled over to me where I was standing with a soft-drink observing the frolicking throng. "You still want to do morning drive?" he asked. "Of course," I replied. "Is this an offer?" "Well," he said, "not exactly. We're going to replace Brian Wilson (who last I heard was a hot-shot talk show host in San Francisco) and you're our first choice. But we need to hear you do the show for a couple of weeks. "Another audition?" I said. "Yep," said Mark, "but this is the one you've wanted since the first day we met."

So I did it. I got up every morning in the dead of winter at 4:00 in the morning and taxied to the station, where I spent an hour-and-a-half reading the papers and preparing my "ad-libs" for the up-coming show, and then went on the air for four hours helming a show filled with special reports—sports, news, weather, traffic, stock market, commercials—to the point that I hardly had a chance to open my mouth! But I guess whatever I did say was good enough, because they offered me the job at the end of the first week.

Believe it or not, I turned it down! I had decided in my first audition week that this gig just wasn't for me. I didn't mind the hours so much, but I didn't enjoy being so limited as to air-time and I'd come to realize that if I did take the job I'd put "Mr. Mother Earth" in jeopardy, and he, after all, was my true bread and butter. I decided that I'd rather keep things status quo and thanked them profusely for the offer.

I have never regretted that decision.

The Producer

As Jimmy Durante (another old-time comedy legend whose signature was his giant nose, thus he was affectionately nicknamed "The Shnozz") used to say, "Everybody wants to get into the act!" It does seem to be true—the minute somebody finds out you're in show-business they have a script to show you, or an idea to tell you, or a daughter who should be in pictures…Every taxi-driver in New York has a screenplay in his trunk…the butcher has an idea for a great sit-com…Very few folks ever walk up to you and say, "I want to be a producer and make a picture. How much money do you need?"

Well, believe it or not, while I was living in New York I actually met one of those people who wanted to be a producer—and I came away $50,000 richer and with a screenplay to boot! I include this story because it's a wonderful insight into far a person will go to become a part of that Biz we call Show.

It was sometime in the early '80s, while I was still living with Page on Perry Street. A friend of mine named Peter Frame had recently come to New York to work on the filming of a Martin Scorsese-Robert DeNiro-Jerry Lewis movie called *The King of Comedy*. Peter and the entire crew of the movie were staying at a fancy west-side hotel, The Mayflower, and Peter, a hugely outgoing sort of guy, soon became the King of the Mayflower Lounge. From almost the moment the movie company arrived and checked in, Peter found his favorite seat in the hotel's upscale bar and proceeded to indulge in his nightly routine which included swallowing as many drinks as he could hold and picking up as many girls as he could handle, in that order.

One night I joined Peter at his table for a bite to eat, and during the main course we were joined by Scorcese and DeNiro, who sat with us long enough to have a drink before retiring upstairs to talk about tomorrow's shooting. Sometime soon after we finished our dessert we were approached by a heavy-set man, a nice-looking guy in his middle-thirties. He walked up to the table and said, "Hi, there. My name is Seth, and I see that you guys know Scorcese and DeNiro." King Peter nodded casually. "I number Marty and Bobby among my closest friends," he said, which happened to be true. "What can I do for you?" "Well," said Seth, "I'm interested in investing some money in a movie, and I thought maybe you could give me some advice." Peter almost lept from his chair and extended his hand to Seth. "Seth, my friend, this is your lucky night!," Peter said. "Please sit down."

Well, for the next couple of hours I pretty much watched in amazement as Peter worked this poor guy like a trout at the end of a fishing line, reeling him in, slowly but surely…His pitch was quite simple: I was the greatest writer in the history of Hollywood, a guy who'd written a passel of pictures and would be our writer—get that? *our* writer!—Peter would produce the picture and Seth would be the Executive Producer. Of course, neither Peter nor I had a clue whether or not Seth really had any money or was just some kind of star-struck nut, but Peter persevered. Even if Seth was a phony it gave Peter a chance to sharpen up his conning skills.

Next thing I knew, Peter was spinning out a premise for a movie which he had decided would be our project. It was a fairly interesting idea about things paranormal with a lot of sex thrown in—and best of all the leading part would be perfect for his very closest pal, "Bobby" DeNiro. Seth was hooked. All that was left was to talk hard business and come up with some hard cash.

We met again the following day in the back yard of my Village "mansion". Seth was duly impressed, but Peter and I still weren't sure about him—he had told us he was in real estate and lived in a big house in Marin County, a very expensive Northern California neighborhood, but we still had no way to know for sure if he was really loaded. In any event, Peter negotiated a deal then and there which included a payment of 50 thousand dollars for the script, to be divided into three installments—Twenty-thousand up front, fifteen-thousand upon completion of the first draft, and the final fifteen on completion of re-writes. Peter would get a stipend for producing and a weekly retainer while we were in "pre-production." Seth nodded and said it sounded like a good deal to him, and he would call us in the next day or two after he had a chance to have his attorney draw up a contract. Upon signing of the contract he'd hand over a check for 20 Gs.

We parted company, and I don't think Peter and I really believed we'd see any money although Seth had certainly seemed like a square shooting guy.

But sure enough, we got the contracts within a week along with the check and I began writing the script in earnest. I admit that I had actually begun to believe that if the script were good enough, Scorcese or DeNiro or both might agree to make it. Stranger things had happened in show-business—that I knew.

The outcome of this story is actually far more colorful and interesting than any screenplay you could write. It's true that truth is stranger than fiction: I finished the first draft of the screenplay and within a week a check for the second installment of fifteen-thousand dollars was delivered to my door. Peter, Seth and I had several meetings on the script, which we all agreed was very good but needed work, and I commenced doing a re-write. About a month went by, and neither Peter nor I had heard from Seth and repeated phone calls to his various numbers were all answered by machines, but we really thought little of it He'd really been excited and felt he was learning how to be a producer (which he was) during the process so far, and he'd already given me forty-thousand dollars and whatever he was paying Peter, so we were sure he hadn't run out.

Finally, the day I delivered the final draft to Seth's lawyer I found out the answer:

Seth was not in real-estate after all, although he did own the giant home in Marin County. He was a drug dealer!—a really big, big, big-time marijuana importer!—and the bad news was he'd just been busted bringing a huge shipment of weed into Hawaii! According to his attorney, he was in jail in Honolulu and would probably be tried there. (I wonder if marijuana has been legalized when you read this. I hope so.) In any event, he was going to be away for a long, long time. (No wonder he'd had these visions of being a big Hollywood Producer—according to his attorney he only dealt in the very highest quality stuff and was a steady user of his own product.)

With all his trouble, however, Seth made good on his end of the bargain and within a few weeks I got the balance of the fifty grand, plus the rights to the script . Unfortunately, Peter wasn't able to interest either Scorcese or DeNiro who had projects lined up into the next millennium— literally.

I submitted it a few times here and there over the years, but never was able to make a deal, although I would classify it as one of the very best scripts I ever wrote.

Know anybody who wants to be a producer?

An Adventure In Hong Kong

I love this story and chances are you will too. When I think back to this particular day, I truly believe it defines exactly who I am—or at least who I was back in 1983, and still believe myself to be today.

It begins one morning when I opened my mail and was bowled over to find a check for $11,000—a royalty payment on *Mother Earth's Hassle-Free Vegetable Cookbook*. Talk about found money.....and within seconds after finding it I knew how I was going to use it. For years I had been dreaming about taking a trip to the mysterious Far East, and this little check was going to pay for me and Page to make that dream come true.

We booked the trip the next day—a fabulous tour that included stays in Tokyo, Kyoto, Singapore, Thailand, Hong Kong, and Bali, and left for our three week sojourn less than two months later. Well, it was a sensational trip—all I dreamed of and more, walking in the Ginza in Tokyo, floating down the river in Bangkok, soaking up the exotic beauty of Singapore, seeing all the incredible sights of Hong Kong (with a side trip to Macao, a nearby island where gambling is king), and finishing up in Bali which truly is the most beautiful place in the world. A hundred wonderful things occurred on that trip, many of them pretty interesting—but the best of them all happened in Hong Kong.

I had made up my mind before we left on our trip that I was going to take in the horse races when we got to Hong Kong. As a long-time degenerate horse-player and race-horse-owner, I had always wanted to see the famous track in Happy Valley. I had read many romantic stories and seen many beautiful photographs of this fabulous emerald-green grass track on which, in the British tradition, the horses run the wrong way around, and I was determined to make that a stop on the trip.

Page decided she'd rather go shopping, so off I went by myself to

Happy Valley on one of the many Hong Kong trains. When I reached the track I was already excited beyond a fever pitch. I sought out the entrance to the fabled Hong Kong Jockey Club—a private turf-club for members only—and was floored to discover I couldn't buy my way in! It really *was* for members only and unlike the average American race-track, no amount of begging or bribing could get me past the gate.

Oh, well—so I'd go into general admission and rub elbows with the peasants, no big deal. Except it *was* a big deal, because it turned out that one had to buy one's tickets into the track back in the City! Nobody had told me about this rather strange rule, but I figured one of the guys at one of the gates would surely let me in for a few Hong Kong dollars. Wrong! I must have tried to bribe at least five guards and not one of them would take my money. Meantime, I could hear the call of the races and the roar of the crowd and I was becoming more frantic by the minute. I'd come all this way, not to mention the hour train ride, and it looked like I was going to be stuck on the outside looking in!

I decided to take one more shot at the Jockey Club. As I approached the entrance for the second time, a very pretty young uniformed woman carrying a clip-board went through the entrance. I ran over and called out to her, and she stopped and came back. "Can I help you?" she asked. "I surely hope so," I said. "I'm Dr. Rapp, and I've come all the way from New York to see a race at Happy Valley. Isn't there some way you could get me in?" "Let me see what I can do, Doctor," she said, and off she went. I had my fingers crossed—for some reason, the doctor bit often worked when trying to make difficult reservations, and by George it looked like it might work again.

I paced around anxiously for almost half-an-hour and was about to give up hope, when the girl with the clipboard reappeared with a nicely-dressed Chinese man in tow. He moved up to me and bowed slightly. "How do you do, Dr. Rapp. My name is Dr. Chen." And he reached out to shake my hand. Oh, God, *Dr.* Chen...I could find myself in serious trouble. He continued: "I have heard the story of your travel from New York, and although it is quite against the Club rules, I'm going to extend a bit of professional courtesy to a fellow Doctor and invite you to be my guest in my box." As we headed through the tunnel which led to the seating area I didn't know whether to laugh or cry, especially when the next thing Dr. Chen said was, "And what is your specialty, Dr. Rapp?" I took a breath, and then I said, "Neurosurgery." I figured, what the hell. Might as well shoot for the moon while I was at it. Dr. Chen was visibly impressed. "My, my," he said. "I am but a lowly dentist." Sensing an opening, I said, "You know, Dr. Chen, we in neurosurgery often observe that we are just the same as dentists—except we work on a different sort of cavity!" And before he could speak another word, I said: "Now would you mind if we didn't engage in any more shop talk? I came here to get away from all of that." He bowed deeply and indicated a finish-line box. "By all means, Doctor, I completely understand. From now on we will relax and enjoy the races." And believe me, we did. I didn't cash any tickets, but I had a truly wonderful time.

As I was getting ready to leave, I thanked Dr. Chen profusely, and then asked him if he could recommend a good and honest jewelry store among the thousands in Hong Kong. I wanted to get Page a little something and frankly, I didn't want to get ripped off. Dr. Chen beamed. "You are in luck, Dr. Rapp. It just so happens that my wife is the manager of the very best jewelry store in all of the Orient." He gave me the address and his card and told me to be sure and tell his wife that he sent me.

On the way home I sought out Mrs. Chen at her very posh jewelry store. I introduced myself as Dr. Rapp, told her about my day with her husband, and after about a half-an-hour of highly personal service, I decided on a bracelet which I bought at a very fair price. I bid Mrs. Chen farewell, and left.

That night, I was telling the story to a group of hugely important American businessmen who were headquartered in Hong Kong. When I got to the part about Mrs. Chen, one of the men practically shouted, "You're kidding! That really is the best jewelry store in Hong Kong, and would you believe I've been trying to get an appointment with that woman for a month to do some business and I've yet to be able to get through?" "Well your troubles are over," I said with an arrogant air. "Just call again and say you're a friend of Dr. Rapp's. I'm sure things will work out just fine."

And here's the punch line: About a month later a big, beautiful basket of goodies was delivered to my front door on Perry Street. Attached was a thank-you card. It was from the aforesaid businessman who had written that thanks to his friendship with "Dr." Rapp, he'd finally gotten to Mrs. Chen and closed a substantial deal. It was the perfect ending to an absolutely perfect story, and one which obviously I will never forget.

Now if you'll excuse me, I've got to see a patient about a brain scan.

"Saturday Morning Live!"

By the end of my third year in New York, I was a firmly entrenched member of the community with lots of prestige, a measure of fame, and a lot of very good friends. I was blessed to become a one of a group of really great people who were the "cast" of a two-hour show at Channel 5 called *Saturday Morning Live*. The show was conceived and produced by Paul Noble, who by now had become my nearest and dearest friend in New York, and it was designed to appeal to all the folks who weren't home at 9 weekday mornings to watch the "service" programs such as AM New York. We had a cook, a fashion expert, an animal expert, a carpenter, a consumer reporter, and me doing the plants. All the other folks were pure amateurs in the media, although each was a true expert in his or her field, but by shrewd casting and divine accident, you never saw such fabulous chemistry in your life. By the time the show had been on just over a year, it seemed that some portion of our program had been seen at some time or another by every living adult in all five boroughs. I could not walk down the street without being recognized by every fifth person who passed me by. People would say hello all day long every day, followed by "Love your show" and sometimes even a request for plant advice which I gladly volunteered. (Once a bum chased me up 7th Avenue and as he approached I was frankly nervous and didn't know what to expect. All was cool, however—he just wanted to ask my advice on how to grow marijuana.)

Saturday Morning lasted for 3 seasons and became a city treasure, but then new management came to Channel 5 and decided our bottom line was too weak so off we went. Paul Noble tried valiantly to make the new out-of-town owners understand that our show was a "loss leader" and made lots of friends for the station and its slate of weekday programs but his protests were for naught. Red ink is red ink and that's the end of that tune!

Bill, Mike, Cyndi, Me, and Ruth of *Saturday Morning Live*

It was sad not to see the gang every Saturday—by this time we had all become hugely fast friends off the set as well as on—but untold more doors were now open to the crazy plant guy who always wore a sweatshirt emblazoned with the name "Mr. Mother Earth" across the front. (Only on TV, not out in public!) I once again felt like a genuine celebrity, and it felt real good! I thought about it a lot…how I'd walked into the city jobless and friendless, and hey, look at me now! They say about New York that if you can make it there you can make it anywhere, and I had made it!

I never stopped being amazed at the constant barrage of recognition I received on a daily basis. People waved from cabs, called out from windows, greeted me warmly in the streets—it really made New York feel like a big, friendly city and I admit I loved every moment of it. One of my biggest thrills came on the day I was walking up 5th Avenue near Rockefeller Center when I heard a female voice calling out "Mr. Mother Earth" from somewhere on the crowded street. I turned around to look, and there, leaning out a cab window and waving at me, was one of my idols—Jane Pauley, then co-hosting *The Today Show*. "You need a ride?" she called, and even though I was almost at my destination, I ran over to her cab. "I'm going up to 86th Street," she said. "Can I give you a lift?" "Absolutely," I replied as I got into the cab. "That's where *I* was headed!"

The gang at Disney World

We had a marvelous conversation all the way up to 86th street in heavy afternoon traffic, and while everybody else on the road was screaming and cursing at the slow going, I was hoping our ride would never end. Alas, it did, and we parted company at 86th and 5th. I took the bus back downtown where I had been headed in the first place.

I often recall a particularly amusing story which features another newsroom icon, Dan Rather. I was coming out of a restaurant on 57th

Street one afternoon just as Mr. Rather was passing by. I fell into step about five or six paces behind him and the two of us proceeded west on 57th. As we walked the long block between 6th and 7th avenues, at least ten people gave me big smiles and spoke their "hello," "love your show", whatever. When we finally reached 7th avenue, Mr. Rather turned around and frowned at me.

"Excuse me," he said, "but should I know who you are? It seems like everybody else in New York does!" I shrugged modestly. "I suppose you should know who I am, being the world's most important newscaster and all. I'm Mr. Mother Earth and I do a gardening show on the radio and TV." And then, because I could feel his insecurity, I added: "And by the way, Mr. Rather—every single person that passed you by turned back and looked and recognized you. But people are intimidated by you so they don't say anything—but I'm just a meager plant guy so they're not afraid to say hello to me."

A wave of recognition passed across the famous newsman's face. "Of course," he said. "I just didn't recognize you without your sweater on!"

For the sake of my ego I chose to believe him.

My Regis Years

I first met Regis Philbin back in the early '70s when he and his lovely wife Joy became customers at Mother Earth. At this point in time Regis was floundering in his career and was still very depressed about his famed contretemps with comedian Joey Bishop. In case you don't remember that little incident, it went something like this: Regis was Joey's sidekick on a national late-night show ala the Tonight Show or David Letterman. One of Joey's favorite pastimes was to insult Regis, to put him down, his cracks usually being more mean than funny. For months and months Regis suffered Joey's abuse, and then one night he finally broke down. Joey trotted out one insult too many—the crack that broke the camel's back—and Regis walked out right then and there. Got up off the couch, said something to the effect of "I quit", and disappeared into the wings. This dramatic exit created quite a stir in Hollywood, and matters became even worse the following week. Regis had a change of heart and decided he wanted back on with Joey, but Joey had a condition: Regis had to get on his hands and knees in front of a national TV audience and beg for his job back. The bad news was that a desperate Regis actually did it, and for quite a while he was an object of ridicule and *persona non grata*. He was doing a weekend show in St. Louis, as I recall, but that was about it for him careerwise. Add to that his continuous sorrow about his son, who was institutionalized with a congenital defect, and Regis was one unhappy guy.

(I must stop here to relate a story which I never told Regis but which probably would give him a good laugh. Back somewhere in the '60s, Joey Bishop was starring in a half-hour sitcom eponymously named "The Joey Bishop Show". Sam and I were contracted to write six episodes, and we labored extra hard on our first show to make the best impression possible. Everybody seemed very pleased with our script, there were a minimum of

145

changes requested, and we showed up at the Friday night taping anxious to hear how everything played. Well, we had a rude awakening that night: During the four days of rehearsal and blocking that preceded that taping *every single line of our script had been changed!* Not one of our jokes remained—not one!—and quite frankly we were really taken aback. We sought out the Producer, a nice guy named Chuck Stewart, and asked him what the hell had happened? We thought they'd liked our script. "Oh, don't take it personally," said Chuck. "Joey does that to every script every week." Somewhat mollified, we went to work on our second assignment and once again took careful pains to deliver the best script possible. And again, come Friday night, not a word of our script remained intact. The third time around we decided we'd had enough, so we did the unthinkable: We handed in a script that consisted of 36 blank pages! "We thought it would be easier if you could just start from scratch," we told Joey, and needless to say were fired on the spot. But thank God we had plenty of other jobs and the feeling we got was worth it.

Interesting post-script to that story: Some years later Lynn and I were called to do the Tonight Show and imagine my surprise when we were told Joey Bishop would be the Guest Host that night. Thankfully, Joey told the story himself and admitted on national television that if he'd have been one of his writer's back then he'd have done the same thing himself. The rest of that appearance passed without incident.)

Back to Regis. He was convinced he would never work again. I remember one night while we were flying back to St. Louis—Lynn and I used to go back and do his show as often as we could—he actually broke down and cried for almost an hour. I comforted him as best I could and assured him that he'd be a big star someday. Little did either of us know...

A few years later, having managed to scrape by with his St. Louis show and a guest-hosting gig here and there, Regis was named host of the ABC morning show in Los Angeles, a really good job that was the beginning of his comeback. I forget who his original co-host was, but when the smoke cleared it was Cyndi Garvey, wife of the former Dodger star, Steve Garvey. It was on this show that Regis perfected the formula that has taken him to stardom on his long-running national morning show. The most important segment was the first 10-minutes of the show which was called "Host Chat." It was in this segment that Regis and Cyndi would chat about their previous evening's outings, the headline news of the day, and any other gossip that came to their minds. This became Regis's trademark, and has used it to good stead to this day with Kathi Lee Gifford and currently Kelly Ripa. The other thing Regis always did was make his producer part of the cast, somebody to whom he could toss the occasional jab (getting even for his Joey Bishop days I always thought) or use to get a laugh. Thus "Gelman" has been impelled to stardom.

Speaking of Gelman, there is one lucky young man. He came to Regis' show in New York as an intern and has been there for the full 20-some-year run of the show, the last 15 or so as the head honcho.

When I first came to New York, they had a morning show very similar to the one Regis was hosting in L.A., but for whatever reason their version just hadn't caught on. Sometime in 1980 Mr. Mother Earth became a regular weekly guest on the show, and I must have worked with at least a dozen hosts that the brass was auditioning. During all those weeks and months, I championed Regis to the powers-that-be. I kept telling them that Regis would save their bacon—he was sure-fire to hit it big in New York if they would only give him a chance. And the good news was Regis was available: At this point in time he had made an unfortunate career move, quitting the L.A. Morning Show and taking on a network gig with co-host Mary Hart that died after 13 weeks and was replaced by re-runs of some sort of scorned sit-com. Regis was out of work again, but I knew he would be perfect for the New York spot.

It was about this time that I got the call from Paul Noble informing me of his plans for the Saturday morning show, so I left ABC and cast my lot with Paul and Saturday Morning. We had been on about a year or so when somebody at ABC finally got smart and Regis Philbin came to New York to host their flailing morning show. His first co-host was once again Cyndi Garvey, and they caught on at once. Cyndi, however, had some issues about money, and when contract time came again, she left when they wouldn't give her equal pay with Regis. After trying at least a couple of dozen women as co-hosts of the show, the producers settled on Kathie Lee Johnson, who had been substituting now and again on *Good Morning, America*. It was a perfect teaming—the chemistry between Regis and Kathie Lee was electric and before long the show was established as a solid hit.

Sometime in 1983 the doors were slammed shut on *Saturday Morning* for reasons I have described earlier, and I was unemployed as far as television was concerned. But not for long. Within a week of *Saturday Morning*'s cancellation, I got a call from Regis. "Well," he said, "you ready to come over with me now?"

Of course I said yes, and thus Mr. Mother Earth began an eleven-year stint with Regis & Kathie Lee. Once a month, every month for eleven years Mr. Mother Earth came onto the stage and presented a lesson in plant care. Sometimes either Regis or Kathie Lee was on vacation, and so I worked with dozens of guest hosts over that span. Some of the more memorable moments occurred with people like the former *Saturday Night Live* star Dana Carvey. It was a morning where I had veered from my usual format and written a sketch to coincide with the Oscar Nominations. I presented my first annual Greenie Awards—Best Performance by a Flowering Plant, Best Performance by a plant in a dark corner, that sort of thing. I got all dressed up in a tuxedo, Kathie Lee had on a glittering Oscar night gown and guest-host Carvey was wearing an oversized tee-shirt and shorts! I had written lines for all three of us, but to say that Dana strayed from the script would be putting it mildly. The result was nearly 20 minutes of continuous hilarity, way too long for a segment on that show, but Gelman couldn't stop us because he was too busy laughing. During those eleven years I passed on quite a bit of really good information—lessons on bonsai, plants from your grocery bag, how to re-pot, cleaning your plants—but that morning with young Mr. Carvey was in a class by itself.

It was very gratifying to have people stop me on the streets once again and tell me how much they enjoyed my segments and how much about gardening they had learned from me over the years. One of my biggest thrills was the day I got into an elevator and found myself alone with one other passenger. It was Jane Powell, a movie-star from my youth on whom I had had an enormous crush, but before I could fawningly tell her how much I had loved her back then, she started to gush at me! Jane Powell, a girl I had dreamed of marrying, was actually telling me how much she enjoyed me on the radio and TV. We wound up going to break-fast together where I finally confessed the story of my love. She thought that was very sweet and when we parted she gave me a big kiss on the cheek. Ah, the perks of being a gardener!

If You Knew Suzie...

My godfather, the legendary comedian Eddie Cantor, had a signature song: He would jump about the stage, white-gloved hands twirling, huge round eyes rolling, and sing, "If you knew Suzie, like I know Suzie, oh, oh, oh what a gal..." Well, here it is almost 70 years later, and now I can call that little ditty my signature song, too. There must be something to this "bloodless genealogy" thing after all. (Huh?)

It was in early December of 1983 that I got a call from my friend and sometimes writing partner Marty Stone, with whom I wrote what I consider the single funniest project I ever had a part in—a little book called *Gifts From Our Garbage* unfortunately long out of print—but a few copies have survived, and luckily my family has them! Anyhow, Marty knew I had recently broken up with Page and was in the market for female companionship, and he boldly announced he had just the girl for me. Her name, he told me, was Susan Stoller, and she worked as assistant to his friend and neighbor, Elliot Hoffman, a big-time New York entertainment lawyer, whose clients numbered Dizzy Gillespie, The Who, Luciano Pavarotti, Cindy Lauper, Stan Getz—did I mention he was a big-time entertainment lawyer?

I wasn't much for blind dates, but Marty's praise for her looks and personality was so long and loud I finally called Susan up and invited her to be my date at a forthcoming surprise birthday party for my best friend Paul Noble. (To this day she marvels at my bravery, inviting a blind date to a party populated by all my closest friends.) She lived in a fashionable doorman building on East End Avenue and 86th Street, right across the street from a beautiful riverside park and just down the block from Gracie Mansion, home of then Mayor Koch (and all subsequent mayors.) Mightily impressed with the address, I rode up to her third floor apartment and

149

rang the bell. Susan opened the door and right away there was good news and bad news: She was great-looking all right, blonde, tiny waistline, great figure…but the apartment reeked from cigarette smoke, one of my major turn-offs. Oh, well, I thought—had I known she was a smoker I probably never would have agreed to the date, and what I thought would be a grand, spacious up-town apartment turned out to be a teeny one-bed-room with a kitchen not big enough for two people at once—but as long as I was here, and she was so darned attractive…

So off we went to the party, and everything Marty had told me about Suzie turned out to be true: She was bright, vivacious, funny, an honors graduate of New York University and a walking encyclopedia of rock and roll music, a genre I knew very little about. But she was also a tremendous fan of Broadway show music and jazz, my favorites, not to mention being hugely conversant about sports, and we really hit it off right from the start. I can't really say it was love at first sight, but it surely was lust, and within a few weeks things began to get really serious. She was still smoking, but by now she was going off to bathrooms and the like, including going outside in the hall in her own apartment building, and I gave her lots of points for that.

I was living in Washington Heights at this time—the very last Man-hattan stop of the A train before it traverses into the Bronx—in a huge apartment I was subleasing from an electrician friend of mine. But with all my giant two bedroom, two bath, step-down living room comfort, I found myself spending more and more time at Suzie's little pad. In fact, some-where about six months after that fateful first date, I decided to chuck the Washington Heights commute and with Suzie's hearty approval, I moved into her place. There was hardly room for the both of us—I remember the most inconvenient feature being the single, tiny bathroom, especially in the mornings when ablutions must be performed—but we were happy none-theless. Things progressed—we fought, we broke up, we reconciled, we broke up, we reconciled—but suddenly, about two years after we first met, I was consumed with the overwhelming desire to propose marriage. I was a bit surprised that Suzie had to take some time to think it over, but to my everlasting good fortune she said yes and plans were made.

We were to be married at Temple Emanuel on Fifth Avenue, the oldest and most historic temple in Manhattan, followed by a dinner at our friend Anne-Marie Huste's mid-town townhouse. Anne-Marie had been the cook-ing member of the cast of Saturday Morning and we had become great friends. She was a very well-known figure in the New York foodie world, having been

Suzie and my wedding day

Jackie Kennedy Onassis' cook before opening the downstairs of her beautiful home as a place for private parties. We had been to several of her dos, and they were always magnificent, so when she volunteered to do our wedding party—the salaries of the waiters and the wholesale cost of the food being our only expenses—we were overwhelmed with gratitude, and of course we accepted her generosity quickly, before she could change her mind.

Unfortunately, there were some problems with Suzie's family prior to the wedding—aren't there always?—and the bottom line was Suzie decided to tell her family that the wedding was cancelled and we were going to elope. We were both very uncomfortable with that decision, but we went ahead anyway, and it was a truly marvelous day.

It began by Suzie getting a professional makeup job as a gift from a very well-known singer, Roberta Flack, and then a limousine ride to Temple Emanuel in a car provided by yet another one of her clients. The ceremony itself in the Rabbi's study was lovely, and the party afterwards was typical Anne-Marie, except even more so than usual. The dinner was incredible—butternut squash soup, choice of veal or salmon, perfectly cooked vegetables, sorbet to cleanse the palate, and finally Anne Marie's famous "Normandie" cake for dessert—the cake, she often said, "that got me where I am today." During the entire party we were serenaded by a wonderful

Julliard-trained violinist whom I had hired after hearing him play in the subway. The guy was sensational! A true concert violinist, he took great pride in his work in the subway, and made a damned good living besides. A couple of years after our wedding, he played a concert in Lincoln Center, and a couple of years later he played the National Anthem at the Mets' season opener! Do I have an eye for talent or what?

Unfortunately, Suzie's brother found out that we hadn't cancelled things after all, and you can imagine the reaction from her mother and father and aunts and uncles—not to mention the damper it put on our honeymoon in New England. For several years there was no communication with Suzie's family. There was a whole lot of anger, but to this day Suzie believes she was justified given all the circumstances, and I quite agree. It's just that I'm not much for confrontations, so I probably would have grit my teeth and let them come ahead and ruin the party. But eventually things got patched up, and all was forgiven on both sides of the fence. Suzie was at her father's bedside when he died of cancer, and after bringing her widowed mother out to California and into a retirement hotel she was her only caretaker until her death about three years later.

Suzie's like that—she's a caretaker, a nurturer. Every day I thank the Lord (or Marty Stone) for sending me a woman who'll get up 15 minutes earlier than necessary to squeeze me a glass of fresh orange juice! Since we moved to California she has become at least as much of a mother to my kids and as much a grandmother to Hannah and Sophie as their biological mother/grandmother, and that's no insult to Elaine. Suzie has created a family that gathers for Passover, and Chanukah, and Breaking the Fast, and Thanksgiving, traditions that had ebbed away during my mother and father's declining years. I'll never forget the look in Hannah's eyes when she was about four-years old, looked around the table, and in a reverent voice said, "Everybody's here!" There is nothing more wonderful than family, even allowing for the inevitable bickering and disagreements, and the older I get the more I realize how true that is.

Suzie and I have been married 17 years as this is written, and I guarantee you we shall stay married until death do us part. She's the best thing that ever happened to me and I will be forever grateful for everything she has done for me and my family. Oh, and by the way—she's long ago quit smoking.

California, Here We Come!

As much as I had come to love New York, and as many friends as I'd have to leave behind, the day came in 1988 when I knew it was time to go home. Danielle was 25 and doing wonderfully well in her career as a retail clothing buyer for a large department store chain; Lisa was 28 and making a bundle of money as an entertainment reporter for the National Enquirer and supplementing that income with frequent appearances on TV and radio; my brother Paul had opened a successful business wherein he videotaped legal depositions; Mom had developed Alzheimer's disease and was in the stage where we beginning to notice the symptoms; and Dad had given up on life and spent most of his days at home in his bathrobe agonizing over having made a fortune and spent it. It just felt like I'd better get on back to Los Angeles before the most important people in my life passed me by.

Although Suzie was a native New Yorker, born and raised on Long Island, she was eager to make the move, thank God. I wouldn't have blamed her if she'd been resistant to leaving everybody and everything that was familiar to her, but by that time her mother and father had moved to Florida, her brother lived in Queens, and her nephew David was a student at Cal Berkeley, so she really didn't feel any incredibly strong ties to NYC.

So on October 12, 1988, just as Columbus had done so many years before, we started out on our California adventure. Suzie had gone out to the Coast without me a couple of weeks earlier to scout for an apartment—a pretty doggone daring thing to do, considering she didn't know the territory. I had laid out the parameters, however—I wanted a nice, big, comfortable apartment somewhere on the West Side, where I had lived my entire California life. With Lisa as her guide and companion, Suzie scouted the area and after a couple of days called and told me she had found it: Eighteen-hundred square feet on Beverly Glen in Westwood, a few blocks from UCLA. Two bedrooms, two baths, huge living room, nice kitchen—she assured me I'd love it so I told her sign the lease!

When I saw the apartment I was overwhelmed. It was everything she said it was and more. In fact, although we've talked over and over about buying something—a house or a condo—as of this date we are still living at that apartment on Beverly Glen.

Suzie took to California-living like a duck to water, and after a couple of weeks I felt as if I'd never left home. About half of the old Nate n Al's gang were still congregating every morning so I rejoined my group; Suzie got a great job within a couple of months, working for entertainment attorneys in Century City, no more than a half-a-mile from our home. And I started commuting to New York on a monthly basis, staying two or three days in order to make my appearances with Regis & Kathie Lee, butter up my bosses at Miracle-Gro and *Redbook*, and have dinner with Paul Noble and maybe a couple of other friends.

Things were going swimmingly. Suzie was making friends and adapting to life in Southern California and I had added the title of Indoor Gardening Editor of the *Los Angeles Times* to my resume. I was also working on the radio at KGIL, and then adding in the monthly sojourns to New York, my plate was full to over-flowing.

In the Spring of 1989 my third cookbook came out—*Fabulous Fish* is the title, and it's the best fish cookbook ever. This is not my opinion, it's a *professional* opinion. You see, I was in Brentano's book store one day about a year after the book came out and happened to be standing in the cookbook section perusing the competition. A woman moved into the section and began to browse, and then she summoned a female store employee who was standing nearby. "Do you know anything about cookbooks?" she asked. The older woman smiled. "I hope so. I'm the cookbook buyer for the store." The customer lit up. "Great. I'm looking for a fish cookbook. Any recommendations?" As I looked on, about to pounce, the buyer reached over to one of the shelves and pulled out—you guessed it—*Fabulous Fish*. "This is the one," she said. "Best fish cookbook I've seen in a long, long time." I was overwhelmed. I couldn't help but say, "Excuse me, but I wrote that cookbook." The buyer and I shook hands and I smiled at the customer. "I'll be happy to autograph it for you," I said, and she smiled back. "Thanks anyway," she said, and handed the book back to the buyer. "I'll think it over." And then so help me Hannah (and Sophie) she walked away and out the door. I looked at the buyer, stunned. Did what I think just happen really happen? To this day I'm not convinced. I mean, given the circumstances, how could she have not bought that book?? I don't know why I felt I had to tell you that story, but I guess it's to illustrate the truism that you can't take anything in life for granted, don't count the money until the check clears the bank, etc. etc.

So anyhow, the publisher of *Fabulous Fish* decided to send me on a five-city tour for the book, and I was both pleased and unhappy about the idea. On the one hand I'd learned long ago that the only way to sell a book is to tour with it—get on every big and little TV and Radio Show and into every published paper in every nook and cranny of these great United States and sell, sell, sell—But on the other hand, there is nothing more stressful than a book tour. In and out of lots of cities in a very short time-span—a day here, two days there…On and off of airplanes, in and out of taxis and/or limos to be shuttled to one appearance after another; putting together and then hauling about the props for your TV appearances—plants and accouterments if it were for a plant book, kitchen stuff and food if it were for a cooking demonstration. Obviously I agreed to the tour—I owed that to the company.

So off I went, and things were frenzied but somewhat under control when I got in Chicago, the third city on the tour. My guide in Chicago was a nice guy who happened to have an in with the people at Wrigley Field, and he asked me if I would like to go see a Cubs game that night—from the Pressbox! How could I refuse? So we went—and the reason I remember what should be just another night, is that while I was climbing the ramp up to the press-box, I got a pain in my chest and could hardly breathe for a minute or two. My guide looked worried—was I okay? Should he call an ambulance? No, I said, I'm okay now…I'm just a little out of shape, that's all…

About two months later, in June. I woke up at 5:30 in the morning, walked sleepily into the bathroom, and suddenly was felled by the greatest pain I have ever felt. I crumpled to the floor, ice cold and dripping with sweat. I knew I was having a heart attack. Believe me, you couldn't confuse this with indigestion. I called out desperately to Suzie, who was sound asleep: "Help, Suzie! I'm having a heart attack! Call 911!" In less time than it takes to type this, Suzie awoke from a deep sleep, grasped the nature of the entire situation, and called 911. She hung up the phone and rushed to my side in the bathroom, and almost at the same time we heard the faint wail of a siren heading our way.

They took me to UCLA where I spent several days in intensive care and then a couple of months at home taking it easy and recuperating. Thank God I lived to tell this tale, but I've always found it very ironic that I left the stresses and strains of living in New York to resume the quiet, laid-back life style in Los Angeles, and what had it gotten me? A heart attack!

Go figure.

A Family Feud

One day in 1990 or '91 Lisa called with another one of her hare-brained schemes: "Let's try out for 'The Family Feud," she trumpeted "We can win a fortune!" *The Family Feud*, in case you don't remember, was (is?) a TV quiz show wherein two families of five competed against each other, each team trying to determine the five or six or seven most popular answers to questions like "What is your favorite ice-cream flavor?" voted upon by a hundred people in various surveys. The winning team comes back the following program and the following program and every night thereafter until they finally lose or drop from exhaustion. Most families never get past the second or third game because there's so much luck involved trying to figure out how a hundred strangers will answer any given question.

At first we thought it was just another crazy Lisa idea. But the more she pushed, the more it sounded like it would be fun. So we put together a team consisting of me, Suzie, Lisa, Danielle, and my nephew Brian and we made our appointment to go in for the "audition."

We got to the show's Wilshire Boulevard offices and were led to a rather large room where lots of families were gathered, waiting their turns to be interviewed. The routine was the same for everybody: One family at a time would go into a separate room where a panel of producers interviewed each person in the family and then played a simulated couple of practice-type games. We passed our audition with flying colors and were told we'd be called as soon as a slot arose.

Weeks went by, then months, and finally, by the time almost all of us had forgotten about it, we got the call: "Can you be here Thursday at 10 a.m.?" That was only two days away, so the team had to be gathered post haste. Luckily, everybody was available except Brian, who had a job he had to take care of, so we substituted Brian's father, my brother Paul. We

Lisa Stanley

were informed they taped 5 shows a day, and depending on how we did, we could conceivably be on all 5 and then have to come back the following day to keep going! There would be at least five families at the taping and if you didn't get on, you would come back the following day at the top of the list.

There were a couple of hours of waiting around doing nothing except being nervous, and then finally they started rehearsing. Every family got to run through the game with one of the producers substituting for the real host—a comic named Ray Coombs. The studio audience was brought in and taping finally began about two o'clock. We were scheduled to be the fourth family up, which meant we'd have to sit through three half-hour tapings at least until our turn came up.

Those three half-hours felt like three and a half years. It seemed like an endless wait as taping was stopped and re-started, questions got fouled up and had to be replaced by new ones. Finally, at about 5:00 our turn came at last.. We were to face a family called The Nguyn Family (pronounced "win") who had already won two games. Well, the Nguyns were the Losers as The Rapp Family trounced them and advanced to the big buck round, "Fast Money," where the pot was ten thousand bucks! Lisa and Paul were chosen to be the Fast Money team, and they had to score at least 200 points for us to get the loot. Do I need tell you they did it with many points to spare? Bless 'em! So The Rapp Family was told to go home and return the next day when we would be first up as the defending champs.

The following day the routine was the same, except we were first up when the taping started. We whipped through our hapless opponents and once again were tapped for Fast Money. Today's pot, 7 G's. Once again Lisa and Paul took the stage, and once again were easy winners. Seventeen thousand dollars, and we had at least one more game to play.

I won't keep you in suspense. We lost the third game and were eliminated, and I will forget the question that did us in: The goal was to find the top five most popular answers to the following question: "What kind of work do teenagers do after school to earn money?" Our opponents had gone first and had only come up with four of the five: Mowing lawns, shoveling snow, baby-sitting, delivering papers…Our job now to win the game and advance to Fast Money was to "steal" the loot by filling in the remaining blank. We conferred, we thought and thought, and when Ray told us time was up, I took a stab at "golf caddie." BZZZZ! Wrongo. We were done. Finished. Washed up in Show-Biz. We shook hands with the victors, said our farewells to the producing staff and picked up our parting gifts of a corkscrew and some cologne and I don't remember what else.

We piled into the car and right away an argument erupted. "We should have got that answer…" "We wouldn't have needed it if you'd come up with that one about the newspaper…" "I tried to tell you the answer would be "not interested…" We were having a real-life Family Feud over who was to blame for us losing. "Wait a minute!" I shouted. "What's going on here? We didn't lose anything. We just won Seventeen-Thousand dollars to split up. Isn't anybody happy?" The bickering stopped and reality struck. We really had been lucky and had a good time to boot. We were on two nights in a row on National TV, and over the years a documentary on the history of the Show has played often and features our appearances! And of course there was the money...

And what was the correct answer to that question we missed about what teenagers do to earn money? "Work at McDonald's." (Any recognizable fast-food place would have been acceptable.) Our friends were amazed we hadn't thought of that, but how could we? Health-conscious snobs that we are—we never go to those fast food places—it just didn't occur to us.

To this day I'm convinced that if we'd just gotten that one question right we would still be playing, and I still get angry about it. If only Paul hadn't missed that one about gemstones, and if Danielle hadn't guessed wrong on the "Name 6 famous Generals" question, and if Lisa hadn't...

There's a sad post-script to this story: Not long after our appearance one the show, Ray Coombs committed suicide—shot himself back in his home-town in the Midwest. I felt sad. He'd been such a nice guy during our stay on the show I felt like he'd become a friend. Who knows why people do things like that? I just hope it wasn't our nattering that did it.

The Travel Section

I have always loved to travel. Some of my most vivid memories are those of my frequent childhood cross-country train trips to Chicago and New York to visit my grandparents. We traveled in the most modern, fastest streamliners extant in those days, the late 1930s and most of the '40s. The Chief, the Super Chief, The City of Los Angeles, the El Capitan…diesel-powered trains that could get you from Los Angeles to New York in 4 nights and three days.

There was nothing more glamorous to me than riding on those trains, which were, parenthetically, an interesting example of a class-system: There were Coach cars where the passengers slept sitting up in their chairs, Pullman cars with curtain-enclosed upper-and-lower berths lining each side of the car, and finally cars with private rooms and teeny little baths. Naturally, my folks always opted for the top-of-the-line private suite, called a drawing room, which was a decent-sized cabin with two pull-down berths and a very small bathroom. Paul and I stayed together in a compartment, which was the same thing as a drawing room only smaller, and there was one more classification: A roomette. I honestly don't remember what made it a "roomette" instead of a "compartment," but it was cheaper, that I know.

The clickety-clack of the train on the track, the extraordinary scenery, the beautiful dining room with its linen table-cloths and fresh flowers and wonderful food (believe it or not), the sound of the Porter's chimes as he came through your car signaling the beginning of meal service…I can hear these sounds and see these sights as if it were yesterday.

Every sleeper car had a Porter. He would be on call 24 hours a day, and his job was to change the sheets on your berths, make sure the bathrooms were tidy and basically see to any other needs like shoe-shines or "room"- service. To insure good service for the trip, everybody would tip the porter generously at the start of the journey and then, depending on the service, add more at the end. (Interesting side-note: All the porters were African-American, or Negroes as they were called back then, before Black became the proper nomenclature. Watch an old black-and-white movie with a train in it and you'll see how these Negroes were portrayed. Largely because of Hollywood stereotyping in the movies, civil rights were still eluding them.) Those were days I wish everybody could have experienced. Certainly, if thought of in today's terms, train travel is virtually a last resort, and of course time tends to add a romantic glow to most nostalgia. But to me, at the time, taking the train was the most exciting thing in the world and I'll never think of it any other way.

* * *

As clearly as I remember the train rides, so do I remember my first plane ride. It was sometime in the late 1930s—'38 or '39, I think, and my father decided to take me with him on an airplane trip to New York. The plane was a Pan American Airlines plane, and because the journey would take 16 or 17 hours counting stops for re-fueling, there were bunks aboard the plane exactly like those in the Pullman train cars! I'll never forget climbing into my bunk at probably about 20,000 feet, four huge propellers roaring, and thinking this was the greatest thing since sliced bread, which, by the way, my generation took for granted.. Naturally, as soon as I was old to enough to understand that flying in a plane had to do with asking a multi-ton steel tube to lift off the ground and then stay there, I have been fairly afraid of flying, basically on takeoff. Even though I have flown over a million miles, I'm sure, I still find myself clutching those seat arms and mouthing "up, up, up…" as the plane ascends. I'll never forget the first time I saw a jumbo jet, very soon after they first came out. It was a 747 destined to fly me to Hawaii, but when I walked into what felt like a hotel lobby, I shook my head. No, sir. There was no way this thing could possibly get off the ground. I tried to cancel out, but a kindly Customer Service person calmed me down and showed me a film of the airplane performing. She finally talked me into taking the chance, and needless to say the flight was uneventful.

* * *

Another "it feels like yesterday" travel memory is the cross-country car trip I took with my dear friend Bill Sawelson a month after we graduated from high school in 1950. I was just barely 16 and Bill was a month away

Me in Japan

from turning 18—I was always the youngest of my friends—and off we went in a 1941 Chevrolet, following a route laid out for us by the Automobile Club that included as many roller coasters as possible along the way. That was the object of the trip, actually—to ride roller coasters as we saw the USA. We were on the road almost eight weeks and had a fantastic time. The Grand Canyon, Albuquerque, Carlsbad Caverns, Old Faithful, The Painted Desert, Galveston, New Orleans, New York City, Chicago, Detroit, Salt Lake City, Las Vegas—we hit 'em all. We were shocked in the South by the ubiquitous separate facilities for "White" and "Colored". Rest rooms, drinking fountains, public transportation, schools—you name it—blacks were definitely second-class citizens, if that. There is nothing uglier than segregation and racism. To read about it or see examples on TV is not the same as being there up close and personal. It was a revelation to Bill and me to see that after almost a hundred years of "freedom", relations between the Confederacy and the Negro had not changed all that much in the 1950 South. Things weren't too hot in the North, either. But the Negroes had no-one to lead them in protest at that time. It was before the days of civil rights laws and Martin Luther King, and for the most part black people accepted their fate with nary a whimper.

So anyway, here are these two teen-age kids armed with a gas credit card and minimal cash, driving around the entire country, staying in motels, eating in diners and the occasional fancy restaurant—and never having

Which one is the Buddha?

a single fear that something bad might happen. It was like that in the '50s. Very Vanilla. Some might say boring, but their are others who suggest those really were the good old days when you could keep your doors unlocked and not be afraid to walk around at night. There were no drugs, except among musicians. Teenage kids had never heard of marijuana, let alone smoked it. And heroin and cocaine, hard-drugs, were strictly an inner-city phenomenon. Most girls were virgins when they got married—quite frequently to their high-school sweethearts—and pre-marital sex for guys was pretty much limited to hookers or women of easy virtue.

As safe as life in America seemed to be, I have still not figured out how Bill's and my parents allowed us to go on that trip!! Can you imagine two kids today making a journey like that with their parents' blessings? I don't think so.

At the wall in Jerusalem

* * *

When I was in high school and college we used to go to Hawaii a lot. A bunch of us had a friend who lived on Oahu in a big, beautiful house, and for $99 bucks round-trip you could fly back and forth. We'd leave on Friday afternoon, get there Friday morning, (it's five hours earlier in Hawaii than in L.A.), leave Sunday evening and get home Sunday night late. I must have made that trip fifty times. I would hope anyone reading this will get to do it at least once. As I write this, Hannah and Sophie have already been to Maui twice—bless 'em. For the ultimate in tropical island experience, however, I'd take Bali ahead of Hawaii. Way ahead. Bali just might be the most beautiful place on earth. Page and I spent four days in Bali at the end of our Far East sojourn, and I don't remember every being in a place that beautiful and serene. I am reminded of Bali every single day, as a gorgeous Batik painting I bought there is hanging on my bathroom wall.

* * *

Sometime in 1967 I got a call from Roger Corman, my producer friend. It was about nine o'clock here in L.A. and Roger was calling from New York. In typical Roger fashion, he skipped the amenities and got right to the point: How would I like to go to Europe and produce a picture for him and American-International Pictures? It was a car-racing picture to star Fabian as a Formula I race-driver, and the plan was to follow and film the series of Grand Prix races in Holland, England, France and Spain. My father and I had just finished writing our play and were looking for a producer, and Sam and I were in the process of splitting up, I was living alone up in the Hollywood Hills, so I was thrilled for the opportunity. "When do we leave?" I asked. "Tomorrow night at 9 o'clock," Roger replied. "So soon??" "You have a valid passport?" "Yes." "Good. Then meet me at 7 o'clock tomorrow night at the TWA terminal at JFK." I made a quick airline reservation to New York for the next morning and after throwing together a couple of bags of clothing I was off to N.Y. I met Roger in the TWA lounge, where he explained that the picture had started shooting already— they had been in production for almost a week and were already two days behind. It was obvious to Roger that the woman whom he had hired to produce this flick wasn't up to the job and he expected me to rescue the operation and put it back on track. I gave him my word I would bring the picture in on budget or under—although he was rich as Croesus Roger was the tightest person I ever knew— and then asked I asked him to give me my ticket so I could go and check in. He handed me the ticket and my eyes widened—it was Coach class! No, sir, I told him, we don't travel Coach, you and I., we go first class! So I marched up to the desk and in a supreme bit of irony made my first piece of work on the picture doubling our travel-cost. Roger grumbled about the added expense, but once we were airborne and leaning back in our big leather seats, he admitted he was glad I'd changed our accommodations.

The picture went well, except for one very trying experience. We were staying in Madrid, filming some scenes in a Flamenco nightclub a few miles from our hotel and on this particular day we would be there from morning till early evening. The first thing I did when we got to the location was to go to a nearby cafe and order up a hundred lunches for the cast and crew—I had about 30 extras that day playing customers in the Club, not to mention the flamenco dancing troupe and several extra musicians. Lunch time came, the owner of the cafe supervised the delivery of the requisite box lunches, we went back to shooting, wrapped things up around 5 o'clock and headed back to the hotel. About halfway back it occurred to me I had forgotten to pay the guy for the lunches. No problem, I figured. We were going to be back there tomorrow so I'd pay him then.

We got back to the hotel and I showered and got dressed, prepared for

A must see in Mexico

a night on the town in Madrid. As I came down the stairs of the hotel, I heard angry voices, and I looked down to see the cafe owner standing in the lobby with two men in suits, pointing up and me and jabbering in Spanish. I realized at once what the problem was, so I continued on down prepared to apologize and pay the bill then and there. There was a problem, however: First of all, none of the three men spoke Spanish, and worst of all, the two men in suits were policemen! This guy, according to the desk clerk who clearly didn't want to get involved, wanted his money or I'd be taken to jail.

Somewhere in Spain

I tried to calm everybody down and took the bill from the cafe owner, only to discover he'd charged me for 125 lunches instead of the 100 that I'd ordered and he'd brought. So I did something very stupid. Instead of simply giving him the extra money which was, after all, not even mine, I started to put up a fight, and the next thing I knew, one of these plain-clothes cops was on the phone and the next thing after that came the sound of a siren. Folks, this was Spain in 1967—Dictator Franco was still in charge, and everybody in the world knew that nobody ever came home from a Spanish jail…Well, when the two jack-booted soldiers carrying machine guns at the ready entered the lobby, I almost passed out with fear. Before I knew what was happening I was being handcuffed and led away, but not before I hollered at the desk clerk to tell me what was happening, and he hollered back they were arresting me for insulting a police officer, a crime just above murder in Franco's Spain.

They loaded me into the back of a vehicle, along with the cafe-owner, and we headed away toward wherever the jail might be. It was at about that moment that I remembered I had contraband in my pocket—a marijuana cigarette and a couple of downers I'd slipped into my pocket before I'd left my room. Ohmigod. If they found those drugs I'd be executed before morning. What was I going to do? My hands were cuffed behind me so I couldn't reach into my pocket…We got to the station, where to my dismay not a single person spoke English, and then I got a really lucky break—they took off my cuffs and threw me into a cell and locked the door behind me without ever going through my pockets. Quickly, I retrieved the joint and the pills and gulped everything down, thus eliminating any chance of being executed—I hoped.

The next thing I knew I was being shaken awake—those pills and that weed had knocked me out cold—and it was morning in the jailhouse in Madrid. Luckily, there was finally somebody there who spoke English, I explained the situation, paid the guy for 125 lunches (this poor shnook, by the way, had been sitting there all night long on a bench, while I was snoozing happily on a cot), and was delivered back to my hotel where after another shower and change of clothes I grabbed a cab and got out to the location.

My first chore, of course, was to order lunch. You can bet I went to a different cafe.

During the course of filming that picture, which was released under the title *The Wild Racers*, I had a romance in Amsterdam, a most fabulous city where at the time I could have easily lived, and in London I had a brief affair with the young woman who was playing Fabian's love interest in the film. It's true about romances blossoming on movie sets. As Alfred Hitchcok once said, "If they're 'kissing' on the set you can be sure they're 'kissing' in the dressing room." But despite my dalliances, we finished shooting two days early and many thousands of dollars under budget, so all in all it was a successful trip. The most exciting thing that happened on that trip, other than my overnight jail stay? While shooting in Haarlem, a lovely little suburb of Amsterdam, I got a telephone call from my father. He'd gotten the financing for our play, and "Match Please, Darling", was going to be produced at the Coronet Theater. I couldn't wait to get home.

* * *

My trip with Lynn to Africa was a wondrous experience. In East Africa we stayed at a series of very well-known game lodges, including the actor Bill Holden's place in Kenya and Treetops, a hotel literally built among the tops of trees, a favorite of Queen Elizabeth I. We spent a few days touring South Africa (before the elimination of apartheid), then went to Kenya, Tanzania and Botswana. I remember when we got to one very fancy lodge they gave us the option of sleeping in a hotel suite or a tent on the edge of the jungle. Interestingly, the tent was more expensive than the suite! Of course we chose the tent because it sounded a lot more adventurous and

A bridge in Prague.

fun. (My father would have chosen it simply because it cost more.) The "tent" was a miniature hotel room—twin beds, lamps, and other comforts, but nonetheless it *was* a tent. We spent the night listening to the sounds of the nearby animals, and marveling at the fact we were actually in *Africa* and decided it was worth every penny of whatever extra we paid.

I expected Africa to look like Tarzan's jungle, but most of the country we drove through was flat—like the enormous animal feeding grounds in the Serengeti or the grassy plains of Ngoro-Ngoro. There we saw zebras, and gazelles, and giraffes, and wildebeests, and elephants feeding on the vegetation We drove to within inches of a sleepy pride of lions, who paid no attention to our jeep—but we were warned by the guide that if we got out, we would be breakfast! We saw hippos and crocodiles bathing in lakes and rivers, and once we saw a leopard, sleeping in the branches of a tree. We saw Mount Kilamanjaro and stood on the equator and wandered through the most primitive of native villages where the people lived in grass huts with only the ground for a floor. We spent an hour hypnotized by the indescribable Victoria Falls. We found really great seashells on the beach at Mombasa, and were surprised at the nature of South Africa's cities—Nairobi, Johannesburg, Capetown—pretty much like California cities—far more developed than I had thought. Trips like this can hardly ever be properly explained. Other than to strongly recommend that if you've got the time and the money, don't miss it for the world. By the way, I've been back to South Africa since apartheid was repealed, and it's a far better place today than it was back then. For everyone.

At one of the Kenyan Lodges, I forget which, we found ourselves hotel mates with the Crown Prince of Abu-Dabbi, one of those incredibly wealthy Arab oil emirates where every citizen—man, woman and child—gets fifty of sixty thousand dollars each year from the government and most of the labor is hired from neighboring countries. Anyway, the Prince rolled in in the lead limousine of a six-limousine caravan—there had been seven of the sleek Mercedes-Benzes when they began their trip, but one had mechanical problems along the way and was left to rot on the roadside. His highness was here in Africa to hunt dyk-dyks, for which privilege he had paid a license fee of $50,000. (Dyk-dyks are teeny, tiny little deer and one of the conditions of the Prince's hunt was he had to shoot from a thousand feet or more, thus severely limiting his kill.) The leader of this safari was a legendary African White Hunter who had recently done a 180 degree turn and had become Africa's Chief Elephant Control Officer. His job was to oversee the culling of the herds to keep the elephant population manageable in ever-dwindling space, and to head up task forces against poachers hunting ivory. (As this is written, a law banning the import of ivory to the U.S. has been in effect for years. Back then it was legal.) I wish I could remember his name, but he was right out of a Hemingway novel. We spent hours listening to him spin tales of his African adventures over the past 60-some years. I cannot predict the fate of the African wild animals, but our White Hunter was not too optimistic about their future. Oh, well. Man is at it again.

* * *

Everybody should go to Israel at least once. Right now, in 2002, I wouldn't risk it, what with Israel and the Palestinians blowing-up each other and innocent by-standers on an almost daily basis. But when Suzie and I went, things were fairly calm. We traveled with a group, as usual, and we had a guide who was truly sensational. He was a native Israeli and had fought for his country in six wars! He was an ever-bubbling fountain of hard information and wonderful personal stories, some funny, some sad. It's really quite an amazing feeling to find yourself at the Great Wall in Jerusalem—the capital of Judaism and Christianity—actually saying prayers and feeling as though they're going to be answered. We saw the spot where Jesus was entombed and then rose up to join his Father. We saw the site of the original Temple, right next door to a magnificent mosque. We marveled at the endless greenery, the citrus orchards and the olive groves where before there had been desert, and we realized why Jews had managed to survive all this time. We saw Roman ruins, we traveled to Masada, where several hundred Jews committed suicide rather than be tortured and killed by invading hordes only a mere few yards away from their mountain-top stronghold. We floated in the Dead Sea which is so loaded with salt you cannot sink, no matter how hard you try. We walked up the same steps as Jesus carrying the cross on his back and wearing the crown of thorns on his head. We shopped in tiny alleyway bazaars where Arabs and Jews mingled in what appeared to be peaceful co-existence. We stood on the banks of the River Jordan. We drove through Bethlehem. There was much, much more—but as interesting as the sight-seeing was, it was a feeling of "being home" that Suzie and I, as Jews, felt most strongly during our visit.

* * *

We have always found that the people who take tours as opposed to traveling alone, are, for the most part, a terrific bunch. Oh, there's usually at least one or two couples in every tour group who are constantly late getting back to the bus, another couple here and there who keep to themselves so you never get to know them, but all and all an adventurous bunch of folks anxious to see the world in which we live. We all start out with that in common, so in a group of twenty or so we always managed to make lots of friends to share meals and free time with. Most of these "tourists" are older folks who have the time and the money to travel, but every now and then we encountered a young couple to whom we almost always gravitated. At the end of a tour you always take everybody's phone number and pledge to keep in touch, but it's like a guided-tour version of Hollywood's "We'll do lunch!" You really never see or hear from your travel partners again. Except on one of our tours we met a really terrific young couple, both of whom were instructors at Indiana University and with whom we had an instant rapport. Their names are Sue and Jim Topp, and we not only kept in touch, we went on tours with them for the next two years after our first meeting, but then Sue and Jim had a much-hoped for baby and our travels together have been temporarily put on hold. Baby Alex is now almost two-years-old and I think the Topps are getting ready to go for another spin. We did Spain, Portugal and Morocco with them one year and Australia the next.

Suzie and I in Moscow

The highlight of the Spain etc. tour had to be Morocco. Talk about exotic! Real snake charmers with real cobras competing for foreign currency in an enormous city square; hundreds of twisting little alleyways, each lined on both sides with booths selling everything from fish to meat to vegetables to clothes for the locals and endless souvenirs for the tourists: And of course there was a stopover in Casablanca where we had lunch in a place called—are you ready?—Rick's Bar. (Humphrey Bogart played bar-owner Rick in an immortal film classic, *Casablanca*. If you've never seen it, now's your chance!) This place was no-where near like Rick's place in the film, but the walls were covered with *Casablanca* memorabilia and it wasn't altogether off the mark.

There were independent , pushy vendors at every sight-seeing stop along the way in Morocco, but that's true in every foreign country we've ever visited. We almost always buy stuff from these vendors and I'm sure we get ripped off more often than not, but we're not talking big bucks and these people need the money worse than we do. My best "shopping" experience occurred in Morocco, where a young man selling beautiful brass plates fell in love with a USC cap I was wearing, and offered to trade me straight up—a plate for the hat. It was one of those rare trades where both sides won!

I made an interesting discovery on that particular journey. One of our scheduled stops was Gibraltar, and I presumed, so help me, that seeing Gibraltar meant parking somewhere and looking out at the famous Rock. Much to my surprise, and I'm embarrassed to admit this, it turns out that on that rock there's a big, beautiful city, filled with shops and restaurants and lots of very expensive homes. There's also a colony of very friendly monkeys at the top of the Rock, where you can be awed by the infinite view of the Spanish coastline and be entertained by the troupe of chatty simians. The population on the Rock is around 30,000—and I'm sure there were that many tourists wandering around the day we were there. Spain and Britain have been arguing for years about who owns Gibraltar, but when were there each country owned a piece of the Rock.

* * *

Suzie and I love to take tours when we travel—we find the conveniences far outweigh any perceived inconveniences. It's really a pleasure to spend a couple of weeks seeing the world while being totally taken care of—no worries about retrieving baggage, or checking into airports or hotels, or driving in foreign places. Yes, there are time constraints which can shorten visits to certain spots or events, but all in all a good tour is like a good buffet—you can fill up by tasting little bits of everything, and for a much better price than you would pay if you booked everything yourself.

We have taken tours to Israel, Australia/New Zealand, Russia/Eastern Europe, and Spain/Portugal/Morocco. On our way to Russia, flying on our own a day earlier than we were to meet our tour-mates in St. Petersburg, we scheduled an overnight stay in Paris. We checked into our hotel at seven a.m., -a lovely bed and breakfast spot only a couple of blocks from the Arc d'Triomphe which was said to have originally been Napoleon's doctor's house—took our bags to our room, then hit the streets not to return until 10 that night. We walked from one end of Paris to the other, from the right bank of the Seine to the left. Past the Louvre, the Ritz, up the Champs-Elysee, through the Tuilleries, around the Arc, dinner at a wonderful little cafe, and finally back to our hotel. We weren't there very long, but then again, we'll always have Paris!

Russia was the antithesis of Paris. Capitalism there was only a couple of years old and the Russians were having a hard time grasping the concept. The economy was in the tank and an organized "Mafia" pretty much ran the country. Hotels were second-rate, and the food fairly awful—but we saw the Bolshoi Ballet perform Tchaikowsky at the actual Bolshoi Theater. We saw a fabulous Russian circus, and we loved a magnificent performance by a troupe of Russian Folk Dancers and balalaika artists. We visited Catherine's palace and the summer home of Peter the Great, and visited Lenin's tomb where Lenin is encased in a glass coffin and looks amazingly life-like, which is not miraculous since it's actually Lenin's body, preserved and re-preserved on a regular basis. We wandered around Red Square in the Kremlin, and met some interesting folks. Interestingly, I think the experience was extraordinary despite the difficulties. We were there, walking on Russian soil, eating in Moscow restaurants. Oh, and of course we bought stuff. We bought stuff everywhere. At some point at a rest stop along the way, one of the many peddlers had a military cap festooned with medals. He asked for seven dollars, I offered five, and he sold it to me. For the next few miles we were all marveling at what a great deal I'd gotten.... Must have been 30 medals hanging from it...And then at the next stop, guess what? Three guys were selling those identical caps for five dollars! Oh well. Not every story can have a happy ending.

As interesting as Russia was, we were glad to head out for Budapest, which turned out to be sort of the Paris of Eastern Europe. We enjoyed a couple of days of sight-seeing, floating down the Danube on a particularly beautiful night, and dined on okay cuisine. Then we moved on to Prague which had its own particular charms. This was the second time Suzie had visited Hungary and Czechoslovakia—the first time was twenty years prior with her mom and dad. That time around the U.S. and the Soviet Union were still in the heat of the Cold War, and things were very, very different behind the Iron Curtain. Night and day, Suzie said, and I can imagine.

*   *   *

Our trip to Australia and New Zealand with Jim and Sue Topp was just as fabulous as all our others with the added bonus that everybody there spoke English! Australia, which was once a penal colony where the worst of Britain's criminals were shipped, is now a continent filled with big, modern cities (Sydney, Melbourne...) and millions of acres of natural land, filled with everything from tropical rain-forests to Sahara-like deserts. Being in the Southern Hemisphere, the seasons in Australia and New Zealand are opposite from ours—December thru March is their summer, etc. One of the highlights during our stopover in Melbourne was the night the Topps and the Rapps enjoyed a truly elegant dinner—while riding around Melbourne on a street-car that had been converted into a first-class restaurant! What a fabulous idea, and we had a ball.

Suzie, in case I haven't mentioned it, has a really bad case of motion sickness—she's got to sit in the front seat of the car, can't deal with bumps on an airplane—so when it came time to take a three-hour boat-ride to the Great Barrier Reef there was no way she could go. It felt like a terrible tragedy at the time—here we were, halfway around the world after 20 hours of flying time in the vicinity of the world-famed Great Barrier Reef and Suzie couldn't go. I hated to do it, but I left her alone at the Hotel and boarded the ship that would take us to the Reef where we could snorkel or dive, or take a glass-bottom boat ride. Sounds great, right? Well, it was a nightmare. The boat-trip was like a three-hour ride on one of those mechanical bulls, but worse yet, when we got to the site of the Reef, we were herded aboard a huge floating wooden raft-like object with chairs and tables and food and drink stands. Said raft was rockin' and rollin' like Little Richard on speed, and there was much seasickness going around. I gamely stripped down to my bathing trunks and tried to snorkel, but I couldn't get more than ten yards from the dock against a very heavy current, which wasn't going to do the trick since the reef was about a half a mile away. I got dressed and got aboard the glass-bottom boat, which was actually a sort of Disneyland submarine ride—a narrow tube, the top half above the water, and the other half below the water where we sat in a single row of seven seats, each with a porthole on each side for optimal viewing. Except I got so claustrophobic after the first couple of minutes of bucking the tides I had to go topside so I never really saw the Reef. When we finally got back to the hotel that evening, I hoped it would cheer Suzie to learn she hadn't missed a thing, but she was already feeling quite cheerful, thank you. She'd found some shops, and, well...

In Sydney we had a special dinner and private tour at the Sydney

Opera House, one of the most famous structures in the world, and spent several hours at the Sydney Aquarium where they had recreated the Great Barrier Reef. The aquarium reef was sensational! Far better than the real thing, based on what I had seen. It extended for about fifty yards and was at least ten-feet tall from floor to ceiling. This man-made display contained several of every single specimen of invertebrate and fish found on the Reef itself. So The Tragedy of the Reef had a happy ending after all.

There are 5 million sheep in New Zealand, and we saw them all. I mean, it's really a gorgeous country and all , but man, there are a lot of sheep. New Zealand, in fact, is the home of "the sheep joke," a joke-genre unto itself. (If you don't believe me, go to the Internet and ask Google or Jeeves to find you "sheep jokes." At last count there were eleven pages!!) There are lots of other wonderful things to see in New Zealand—glaciers, rivers, waterfalls, forests. It's pretty much all about the scenery. The best advertisement for Kiwi-land is a couple I've known for years, Sally and Lew Jarvis. They have gone to New Zealand in January every year for 25 years where they rent an RV and travel around the country and the coasts. I didn't love it *that* much, but we had a really good time. Oh, did I tell you the one about the farmer and the sheep who…

* * *

Although we love to take the more exotic trips, we've also gone on a couple of tamer adventures in the good old U.S.A. and our Northern Neighbor. We thoroughly enjoyed our drive up to Seattle and then our boat-rides across to Victoria and Vancouver in Canada. We had a particularly good time driving from Los Angeles through Arizona and New Mexico to Denver and then home, staying at a fabulous resort called Broadmoor, a hugely grand hotel with a gorgeous golf course and an ice-skating rink where many Olympic champions practice. I'll never forget our visit to the Broadmoor, where we were "comped" thanks to the Colorado Tourist Commission. I played a round of golf in the most beautiful weather you can imagine, and then the next morning, upon which we were to leave there was a blizzard which made travel out impossible. The Hotel, to express it's sorrow at having upset our plans, gave us our suite for another day, along with champagne, flowers, a fruit basket, and free dinner that evening in their four-star restaurant.

* * *

No summary of my travels would be complete without the inclusion of my regular summer visits to a place that's about as mundane as one could imagine but which, for me, holds 60 years of fabulous memories.

Del Mar, California. Seventeen miles north of San Diego, Del Mar is a bedroom community and also a summer resort. It's a city today, but it was just a tiny hamlet back in 1938 when Bing Crosby and a group of his Hollywood friends opened up a race-track. Within a couple of years Del Mar was a summer destination for lots of Tinseltown's beach-and-horse lovers, including, of course, my father. Once Dad discovered the existence of Del Mar, in 1940, it became our summer destination every year thereafter, including this past summer of 2002. I know I must have missed a summer here and there along the way, but for all intents and purposes I have spent at least a week in Del Mar for the past 62 years! Bing Crosby recorded a theme song for Del Mar many years ago that they still play at the start of every race-day. It goes like this: Where the turf meets the surf down at old Del Mar, take a plane, take a train, take a car…there's a winner in each race, and a smile on every face, where the turf, meets the surf, at Del Mar. And then the bugler's Call to the Colors. To this day I tingle when I hear that anthem at our yearly visit to the track.

Through all my school years my parents would rent a house or an apartment for the entire six-week duration of the race meeting. Then for several years we shared a two-unit beachfront apartment building with Jimmy Durante and his family, and then, as my parents' fortunes began to diminish, it became a little house inland about a quarter of a mile, then an inland apartment, and finally a room at the Del Mar Motel.

Actually, the Del Mar Motel is the best place to stay. A few years after the track first opened and they had built a grand hotel nearby called the Del Mar Hotel, the hotel's owners realized their place wasn't big enough so they built an annex right on the beach. It's a two-deck rectangle with about 40 rooms and because of the way it looks and it's raison d'etre, it came to be known as "Alcatraz." If you were consigned to "Alcatraz" you were looked down upon as being strictly "B" list. But by the time I was in my 20s and my parents had run out of housing for me and my family, I stayed in the Motel and realized it had one extraordinary benefit which made it rise above any of the other fancy hotels: It was the only hotel right smack on the beach! Starting from the time they were born, Lisa and Danielle spent their summers in Del Mar, along with my brother's son, Brian. We went every year, and Suzie and I still do. From spending entire summers to spending a week, no matter. The beauty part is that in all those years, nothing has changed—"Alcatraz" is exactly the same (still no cable TV!), and the view of the ocean is exactly the same, and lots of the buildings are the same—makes it real easy to conjure up memories you can practically reach out and touch.

You can pile up a lot of memories in 62 years. And it's amazing how many of them are so vivid I could swear they just happened yesterday. It was in Del Mar that I fell in love for the first time—her name was Judy and she was 14-years old to my 15. She went to Beverly High, and I gave her my letterman's sweater (Varsity football manager, remember?) and we "went steady" for almost two years. When we broke up I was broken hearted, but about two weeks later a deliciously buxom young freshman named Amy put it back together again. Since that wonderful summer with Judy, I've had a lot of girl-friends—but the signal that it was "the real thing" would be an invitation to Del Mar. There weren't many of those, believe me. Judy, my college love Nancy, my New York companion Page, and my beloved wife Suzie. That's my story and I'm stickin' with it!

For several years we owned race-horses and our trainer, Red McDaniel, used to let me exercise them once in awhile down at Del Mar. I had ambitions back them to be a jockey—I was 14-years old and still only five-feet tall and weighed about a hundred pound—but my dreams were dashed when my parents sent me for hormone shots and I sprouted up to the 5'10" fatso I am today. It's just as well—one summer I fell off a fractious thoroughbred and broke my shoulder and reminded me just how dangerous being a jockey could be. I have always like to roam around the backstretch of the race-track, however, and have managed to make that a part of every summer's visit. We get up around 5:30 and head over to the track, where the horses are engaged in their morning workouts. They're beautiful to watch as they gallop around the track, and it's fun to eat in the cafeteria with the jockeys and trainers and exercise people…there's something about the entire atmosphere that just turns me on. Hail to Del Mar—and I sure hope the family keeps up the tradition!

* * *

Now it's 2002 and we may yet take another really long, exotic trip—but for now and forever, if I had my choice to go only one place, you know where it would be? Foster City, California, to my fabulous little Hannah and Sophie! How's that for Poppy love?

Home Sweet Home

We've been back in Los Angeles for 14 years now. The time has gone by faster than any one period of time I can ever remember. During those 14 years I had a heart attack, Mom died of Alzheimer's disease at age 85 and dad died a couple of years later of tiredness at age 88. When Dad died he was honored with a half-page obituary in *The New York Times* and a similar remembrance in *The Los Angeles Times*, but the most touching tribute came a couple of days after he died as I was driving down Wilshire Boulevard listening the radio. A wonderful program on National Public Radio called "All Things Considered" was on, and suddenly I realized they had just started a story about somebody who we had just lost who had contributed so much to the humor history of our country. In an instant I knew it was Dad they were talking about, and I pulled over to the curb to listen. They played snippets of the Bickersons and snippets of Snooks, and at the end of a simply beautiful tribute, they signed off with a song that goes, "We'll meet again, don't know where, don't know when…" That was the first time since he'd passed away that I cried.

For the first few years of our return to L.A., I made a monthly commute back to New York where I would do my thing with Regis and Kathie Lee and visit friends, usually a three-day trip. These jaunts were sponsored by Miracle-Gro, for whom I was a paid consultant, but when our ten-year relationship ended in 1995, I stopped making those trips back to N.Y. Too much stress and no profit, and besides, I was beginning to feel that Mr. Mother Earth had just about run his course after 30 years of campaigning for the Greening of America. I had spawned lots of competitors over the years, gardening information was now available everywhere you turned, and Mr. Mother Earth after all, had had an amazing career. So I pared back my "earthing" to a column in *The Los Angeles Times* and a Saturday spot on radio station KGIL.

Cap'n Phil the Phisherman

I spent a lot of time playing golf during those years, but my game has recently gone 'bye-bye. Even though I have completely lost my swing and am now struggling to break 100, I still in enjoy going out for a round of golf with the guys. I read a lot, and in 1996 I took up water-color painting. It was something I seemed to have a natural gift for, and over the years I have won several blue ribbons in some fairly prestigious art shows. I haven't been painting lately, but as soon as I run out of writing projects I'm going to take out the brushes again. Some of my happiest hours during the last couple of years have been spent painting with Hannah, who has a great natural gift. I hope she will continue with her art for a long time to come.

Just after I lost my job at KGIL when they changed their format, I began to seriously ponder retiring "Mr. Mother Earth" for good. My decision was made for me the day I got a call from a friend of my daughter Lisa who asked me if I would like to come to work as a writer/producer on a new reality show called "Real TV". The pay was almost $2000 a week , the job was a piece of cake, and at 63 years old I was back in show-business. The job of a producer/writer on that show was to look at video-

Danielle the baby bathing beauty

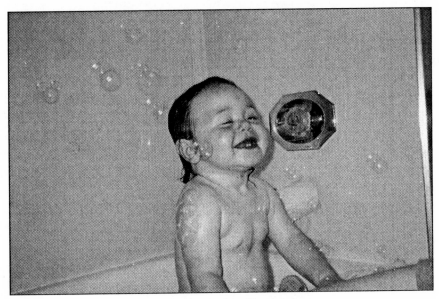

Hannah - like mother, like daughter

tapes of various real events—mostly car crashes, police chases, or other violent happenings—and shape that videotape into a two or three-minute story. So I jumped at the opportunity, and when I showed up for my first day at the office, found myself not only the oldest person among the almost 100 people that worked there in various capacities but old enough to be father to most of them! It was a great feeling finally to be the oldest and wisest in the group, and the kids there really made me feel welcome. They nicknamed me "Old Dog" and all the other writer/producers came to me frequently for advice. It was basically the first time I'd ever had a job where I had to go to work in an office (owning your own business doesn't count) and I actually had a very good time. The gig lasted two years, and was one of the highlights of my waning career.

By this time I had reached "retirement age", which statistically is 65-years-old. That landmark birthday was celebrated at a surprise birthday party which Suzie arranged, where I was truly touched to see friends who had flown in from New York and my high-school friend Bill Sawelson and Danielle and Michael and baby Hannah who was just a doll all evening!

The last few years, with the exception of a couple of scripts I churned out for my old friend Roger Corman, who is now 76-years old and producing really, really low budget movies that go straight to video. you might say I have been retired, or you might say I've been unemployed. I prefer "unemployed" for a couple of reasons: I would take a job in an instant if somebody offered, and I don't believe a writer ever retires, any more than does a painter or a musician. You tend to keep doing your art until you are just not physically or mentally able, hoping, of course that you can sell something you are producing. A couple of years ago I wrote a screenplay with a young fellow I met at Real-TV that won 6th place in a Scriptwriting Contest that had attracted over 2500 entries! I have also written a novel, which I will begin re-writing as soon as I finish these memoirs, which is almost, so I know I'll have a project waiting in the wings.

If I had the strength, I could probably think of another couple of dozen stories that would illuminate my life and the times in which I live. But if you've read this far I would think you have gotten the general idea by now and most likely have had a pretty good time.

And as for you guys, Hannah and Sophie, if anybody asks you to tell them about your Poppy, refer them this "book." I wrote it for you.

The Lawrence family – Sophie, Michael, Danielle, and Hannah.

Index

African Queen, The, 109
Altman, Robert, 53
Ameche, Don, 12-14
Arnaz, Desiree (Lucie), 111
Arnstein, Nicky, 28
Auntie Mame, 112
Baby Snooks, 9, 27-29
Ball, Lucille, 95, 111-113
Battle of Blood Island, 64
Beatles, The, 1
Belasco, Bill, 51-53
Belous, Leon, 43
Bennett, Joan, 63
Benny, Jack, 73
Berle, Milton, 1, 6, 12, 31-33, 77-78
Berle, Ruth, 113
Berman, Shelly, 59
Bernheim, Bunky, 35
Bickersons, The, 12-15.56, 181
Bilko, Sgt., 63
Bishop, Joey, 145-147
Black-Foxe Military Institute, 37
Blake, Whitney, 15
Bogart, Humphrey, 173
Borgnine, Ernest, 69-70
Broadmoor Hotel, 177
Brooks, Mel, 53
Brown, CC, 23
Brice, Fanny, 9, 14, 21-29
Bruce, Kitty, 59-60
Bruce, Lenny, 59-60

Burns, George, 6
Burr, Raymond, 85
Burton, Jay, 77-78
Bush, George W., 4
Buzzi, Ruth, 95, 99-100
Caesar, Sid, 53
Caifano, Marshall, 56-57
Cantor, Eddie, 6, 10-12, 25-26, 149
Carr, Vikki, 95
Carson, Johnny, 77, 99, 105-106
Carvey, Dana, 148
Casablanca, 173
Cass, Mama, 95
Cassidy, Hopalong, 22
Cassidy, Jack, 31
Chez Paree, 56
Ciro's, 17
Clinton, Bill, 4
Cohn, Harry, 17-19
Cookson, Johnny, 23
Coombs, Ray, 158-160
Compulsion, 64
Corman, Roger, 61-62, 65, 165-166, 184
Crawford, Joan, 86
Crosby, Bing, 178
Crossroads, 51
Cuddy, Page, 125-128, 137-139, 149, 179
Cukor, George, 86-87
Dallas, 3, 37

Day, Doris, 71
Decker, John, 27
DeNiro, Robert, 133-135
DeRoo, Ed -43
Donahue, Phil, 107
Douglas, Michael, 95
Douglas, Mike, 107
Dragon, Carmen, 14
Duke, Patty, 77
Durante, Jimmy, 133, 178
Eisenhower, Dwight, 2, 48
Epstein, Elaine (Rapp), 63-64, 152
Epstein, Jon, 52, 77
Epstein, Larry, 64
Erwin, Stu , 83
Erwin, Stu, Jr., 83-84
Fabian, 166, 169
Fabulous Fish, 154-155
Family Feud, The, 157
Flack, Roberta, 151
Forrest, Robert, 31
Frame, Peter, 134-135
Freedman, David, 9-10, 25-27
Friedberg, Billy, 53-54
Gable, Clark, 81-82
Gans, Ron, 59-60, 62-63
Gardener, Ava, 81
Garson, Greer, 86
Garvey, Cindy, 146-147
Garvey, Steve, 146
Gates, Bill, 4
Gelman, 147-148
Gifford, Kathie Lee, 146-148
Gifts From Our Garbage, 149
Gillligan's Island, 65-66, 77
Gleason, Jackie, 15
Gordon, Gale, 111
Grant, Bob, 37
Grauman's Chinese Theater, 23
Gray, Barry, 131
Greene, Robert L., 99-100
Greene, Shecky, 79-80
Griffith, Andy, 78
Hackett, Buddy, 59
Hagman, Larry, 37
Haldeman, Bob, 44

Hart, Mary, 147
Hawn, Goldie, 99
Hefner, Hugh, 56, 71, 88
Hellman, Jack, 18
High School Big Shot, 43, 61
Highway Patrol, 52
Hitching Post Theater, 22-23
Hoffman, Elliot, 149
Holden, Bill, 169
Holm, Eleanor, 28
Honeymooners, The, 15
Hope, Bob, 6, 25, 49, 65, 71-72, 77
Hudson, Rock, 95
Huste, Anne-Marie, 150-151
Huston, John, 109-110
I Dream of Jeannie, 37
Ironside, 85
James, Harry, 39
Johnson, Lyndon, 3
Jolson, Al, 12
Jones, Candy, 131
Jones, Jennifer, 97
Jones, Shirley, 31
Judy, 179
Julian, Artie, 77-78
Jurado, Katy, 70
Keko, Bill, 99
Kennedy, John, 2, 21
Kennedy, Robert, 21
Key Largo, 109
King, Martin L., 163
King of Comedy, The, 133
Klein, Larry, 77
Knotts, Don, 78
Krantz, Judith, 123
Lachman, Mort, 71
Lamarr, Hedy, 81
Lang, Jennings, 65
Langford, Frances, 12, 14
Lawrence, Danielle (Rapp), 26-27, 64,
    153, 157, 160, 178. 183-184
Lawrence, Hannah, 4, 64, 179, 182-183
Lawrence, Michael, 184
Lawrence, Sophie, 4, 64, 179
Laugh-In, 99 Lee, Michele, 95
Leigh, Vivian, 86

Letterman, David, 145
Lewis, Jerry, 133
Lewis, Shari, 103
Little, Rich, 82
Llolobrigida, Gina, 106
Locke, Sam, 53-54, 65-69, 71, 75, 145, 166
Lockhart, Milton, 39-40
Malcolm, David, 54
Maltese Falcon, The, 109
Ma Maison, 115-116
Maraji, Guru, 118-119
Marks, Larry, 87-89
Marks, Nora, 87-89, 106
Marshall, Johnny, 56
Martin, Dick, 99
Martin, Mary, 37
Marx Brothers, 6
Marx, Harpo, 12
Mason, Mark, 129-132
McHale's Navy, 65-66, 69, 77
Mother Earth's Hassle-Free Indoor Plant Book, 121
Mother Earth's Hassle-Free Vegetable Cookbook, 121
Mother Earth's Vegetarian Feasts, 122
Meredith, Scott, 123
Minelli, Liza, 99
Miracle-Gro, 154
Montgomery, Robert, 95
Montaigne, Ed, 65
Morgan, Frank, 12-14
Mother Earth, 83, 121
My Favorite Martian, 93
Musso-Frank Grill, 1
Nancy C., 179
Nate 'n Al's, 77-78
Negron, Chuck, 97-98
Negron, Paula, 97
Neibold,Long John, 131
Nicholson, Jack, 99
Nixon, Richard, 3, 44
Noble, Paul, 128, 141, 149, 154
Odd Couple, The, 75
One Life to Live, 1
Paley, William, 14-15

Paul, Lynn, 78
Pauley, Jane, 142-143
Pepper Young's Family, 1
Pete & Gladys, 53
Peter Loves Mary -53
Peter the Great, 175
Philbin, Regis, 145-148
Powell, Jane, 81, 148
Presley, Elvis, 2
Price, Frank, 84
Prizzi's Honor, 109
Puck, Wolfgang, 115-116
Raphael, Sally Jesse, 37
Rapp, Blanche, 25
Rapp, Brian, 157, 178
Rapp, John, 10, 25-26, 48-49, 71-72
Rapp, Lynn, 79, 86-91, 99, 101-103, 105, 116-121, 127-128, 146. 153, 169, 178
Rapp, Mary, 7, 10, 17-19 , 75, 127, 153, 181
Rapp, Maurice, 7
Rapp, Paul, 10, 18, 75, 127, 153, 157, 159-161
Rapp, Philip, 1, 2-15, 17-19, 25-26, 27-29, 31-33, 73-76, 127, 153, 170, 178, 181
Rather, Dan, 143-144
Real TV, 182
Redbook, 154
Reed, Donna, 66, 27
Rickles, Don, 59, 104-106
Ripa, Kelly, 146
Rogers, Roy, 22
Roosevelt, Franklin, 21, 39
Rose, Billy, 27-28
Rose-Marie, 31
Rose, Si, 66-68
Roth, Philip, 61-62
Rowan, Dan, 99
Rubin, Benny, 7
Rubin, Marvin, 103, 126
Sahl, Mort, 59
Saint, Eva Marie, 72
Sassoon, Vidal, 117
Sawelson, Bill, 162-164

Saturday Morning, 141-143
Scandore, Joe, 104-106
Schwartz, Sherwood, 65
Scorsese, Martin, 133-135
Scovil, Jack, 123-126
Sheinberg, Sid, 85
Shore, Dinah, 103-104
Shubert, Lee, 31-33
Silvers, Phil, 65
Simon, Danny, 53-54
Simon, Neil, 53
Simon, Norton, 97
Simpson, O.J., 21
Skolsky, Sid, 70
Sloane, Larry, 101
Snodsmith, Ralph, 129
Stanley, Lisa (Rapp), 64, 120, 157-160, 182
Stewart, Chuck, 146
St. John, Jill, 71
Stoller, Susan, 113, 149-155, 157, 171-179
Stanwyck, Barbara, 86
Stone, Marty, 149-150, 152
Stork Club, 28

Struthers, Sally, 95
Tarcher, Jeremy, 102-107, 123
Taylor, Elizabeth, 35, 86
T-Bird Gang, 61
Terrail, Patrick, 115-116
Three-Dog Night, 97
Tinker, Grant, 84
Tonight Show, The, 105-106
Topp, Alex, 172
Topp, Jim, 172, 175-176
Topp, Sue, 172, 175-176
Touhy, Roger, 55-57
Towne, Robert, 62
Turner, Lana, 81
Wanger, Walter, 63
Wild Racers, The, 169
Wile, Shelly, 53-54
Williams, Esther, 81
Williams, Robin, 49
Wilson, Brian, 132
Wright, George, 31
Wyman, Jane, 86
Ziegfield Follies, 9, 27
Ziv Productions, 52

The Bickersons Scripts

Volume 1 & 2

Available now from

www.bearmanormedia.com

Buy the original recordings at

www.bickersons.com

BearManor Media

OLD RADIO. OLD MOVIES. NEW BOOKS.

BearManor Media is a small press publishing Big books. Biographies, script collections, you name it. We love old time radio, voice actors and old films.

Current and upcoming projects include:

The Great Gildersleeve

The Bickersons Scripts

The Baby Snooks Scripts

Information Please

The Life of Riley

The Bickersons

The Ritz Brothers

Paul Frees

Daws Butler

Walter Tetley

Don Ameche

Guy Williams

Jane Kean

Joel Rapp

Albert Salmi

Peggy Ann Garner

and many more!

Write for a free catalog, or visit
http://bearmanormedia.com today.

BearManor Media
P O Box 750
Boalsburg, PA 16827
814-466-7555
info@ritzbros.com

Printed in the United States
16759LVS00005B/130-246